Critical Theory and the Teaching of Literature

Critical Theory and the Teaching of Literature

Proceedings of the Northeastern University Center for Literary Studies

Vol. 3, 1985

Stuart Peterfreund, Editor

Department of English, Northeastern University
360 Huntington Avenue, Boston, Massachusetts 02115

Distributed by Northeastern University Press
272 Huntington Plaza
360 Huntington Avenue, Boston, Massachusetts 02115

© Copyright 1985, Department of English
Northeastern University

Library of Congress Cataloging-in-Publication Data
Main entry under title:

Critical Theory and the teaching of literature.

(Proceedings of the Northeastern University Center for Literary
Studies; v. 3)
Papers presented at three symposia on the topic The critical theory and
teaching of literature, sponsored by the Center for Literary Studies of
Northeastern University, in 1984-1985.
Includes bibliographical references.
1. Criticism — Congress. 2. Literature —
Study and teaching — Congresses. I. Peterfreund,
Stuart. II. Northeastern University (Boston, Mass.).
Center for Literary Studies. III. Series.
PN80.5.C74 1985 801'.95 85-63308
ISBN 0-930350-84-7

Table of Contents

Preface

In 1984-1985 the Northeastern University Center for Literary Studies chose as its subject "Critical Theory and the Teaching of Literature." The speakers at the three separate symposia held during that year were Professors Christopher Ricks, King Edward VII Professor, Christ's College, Cambridge University; Robert Scholes, Department of English, Brown University; and Richard Ohmann, Department of English, Wesleyan University. Professor Stephen Owen, Department of East Asian Languages and Civilizations, Harvard University, responded to Professor Ricks; Professor Susan R. Horton, Department of English, University of Massachusetts, Boston, responded to Professor Scholes; and Professor William E. Cain, Department of English, Wellesley College, responded to Professor Ohmann.

The topic suggested itself as a logical consequence of the symposia held during the two previous years of CLS's existence. In the first year of symposia, the subject of which was "At the Boundaries," the attempt was to assess the manner and extent to which the theoretical upheavals of the seventies had altered the presuppositions and practice of "doing" literary criticism. Moving from the more nearly pure and virtuoso to the more nearly applied and analytic, the CLS chose as its subject for the second year of symposia "Literary History: Theory and Practice," in the attempt to explore the impact of theoretical and critical change of the more traditional practice of "doing" literary history. The basis of "doing" theory, criticism, or literary history is, in most instances, an academic appointment, which usually carries as one of its principal responsibilities a substantial commitment of time and effort to classroom teaching. It seemed only natural, then, as the logical consequence of the first two years of CLS symposia, to move from the study to the classroom in order to assess the impact of the theoretical upheavals of the seventies on "doing" the teaching of literature.

Perhaps because teaching is not subject to the same institutional norms or peer review and editing that characterize literary criticism and literary history as they pass from the originating scholar to the scholarly audience, the sort of virtual consensus of focus that characterized the first two volumes of CLS proceedings is not readily evident in this third volume. There is no shared fascination with Derrida and his implications for "doing" literary criticism, as there was in the first volume—although positions taken and held on Derrida underwrite the positions taken and maintained by Professors Ricks, Scholes, and Ohmann. Nor is there a shared belief in a common, irreducible element as there was in the second volume, which elicited a consensus on literary history as a process of telling stories that might be privileged as "better" or "worse" according to their explanatory power and adequacy. However, the nearly exclusive focus by all three speakers on modernist and post-modernist texts suggests that all three speakers view the problematics of teaching literature as connate with the incorporation of modern litature in the university curriculum in the last years of the nineteenth century and first years of the twentieth. Unlike classical and "oriental" literature, which exist in a relatively stable canon and are written in "dead languages" no longer undergoing change and evolution, modern literature is not a fixed entity: its canon changes as the culture that addresses and interprets it changes, and the distance at which interpretation takes place is constantly shifting as a function of linguistic change. Whereas it is possible to gauge one's ideological distance from the classical past on the basis of the relative fixity of that past as a point of departure, it is far more difficult to gauge one's ideological distance from some point in modernity. Like Donne's famous compass, the "fixed foot" of which "makes no show / To move, but doth, if th' other do," the exercise of attempting to gauge one's ideological distance from some point in the modern past must needs suffer from the sort of parallax and distortion of both points, the would-be moving foot and the would-be "fixed foot," moving at once. And yet this distance must in some manner be acknowledged by the classroom teacher and reckoned with as a matter of pedagogical strategy if that teacher is to provide students with an understanding of the distances separating them from the text as an historical artifact, and a means of negotiating those distances in order to establish the sort of understanding that arises from an awareness of the conditions under which the reader-text relationship is possible and practicable across time and distance.

For all three of the principal speakers, the problem comes down to one of determining the status of ideology as the distance separating the reader—especially the relatively inexperienced student reader—from the text. For Professor Ricks, critical theory would appear to be the vehicle of the very ideology that must distance the reader from the text and alienate that reader from it. He grants readily enough that "literary study should be instinct with social and political judgments," but prefers to see these judgments made as a matter of what he calls, borrowing the term and its context from Gerard Manley Hopkins, "principle." It is Ricks' judgment "that the world in which we live is...imperilled by falsity of feeling, so that it is as much as responsibility of the artist and teacher to bring people to understand *illusions* of feelings as feelings." Principle in the critical praxis of Ricks is Occam's razor, dividing the illusory from the real, the theoretical (and ideological) from the true.

Professors Scholes and Ohmann are somewhat less uneasy with the status of ideology. Drawing on the previous work of Roland Barthes, Scholes does not comment of the effects of ideology per se, but rather emphasizes the means of its dissemination: codes. Focusing on Ernest Hemingway in general and the short story "Mr. and Mrs. Elliot" in particular, Scholes argues for a classroom praxis in which the teacher functions as a master cryptographer, proposing not only the semiological status of the text as encoded artifact, but also the particular codes that might be operative in a given instance. For Scholes, the identification of operative codes and the subsequent process of decoding are the basis of literary interpretation. As one accumulates the data of interpretation, the outlines of the ideology that predisposed the author to the selection of specific codes and uses of those codes re-emerge from the text. It is at this point that the student (or the instructor) passes from the realm of interpretation into the realm of criticism, in something like the Arnoldian sense of that term, not only engaged in elaborating the ideology deployed and encoded in the text, but in articulating a critical response to that ideology. Whether as revealed in a testimonial advertisement for Ballantine Ale, or as revealed in his fiction, Hemingway's ideology remains the same, according to Scholes—"in exactly the same complicity with culture" and subject to scrutiny "with the same critical eye."

Professor Ohmann approaches the teaching of literature from a marxist and feminist nexus of theory and concern. For the sake of brevity, he limits himself in the present instance to a demonstration of how the marxist element of his approach allows him, through the use of written "non-lectures" distributed as material supplementary to assigned reading, to suggest the manner in which the ideological forces of a given historical moment serve to determine the social focus, if not the political position, of a given text. As is the case with other versions of this approach from Lukacs onward, it is more nearly apposite to the study of fiction than poetry, and Ohmann's textual base is modern American fiction in this instance—most especially that written between the two World Wars. Ohmann's strategy is to teach criticism (in a marxist sense of the term) by example: his "non-lectures" serve as tangible, documentary evidence—although only as one possible instance of such—of what it means to "do" criticism. Armed with this instance and the substance of their primary reading and lecture—discussions, Ohmann's students work in small discussion sections to produce critical responses of their own, which may range from a retrieval and ideological analysis of other cultural artifacts of the period to the sort of criticism modelled by Ohmann in his "non-lectures." At its best, the methodology that Ohmann uses validates the critical theory underlying it, producing the sort of critical engagement that allowed teacher and student alike to extend the resources of criticism to the analysis of their own ideological presuppositions. "And, as Marx would have it, the educator got educated." It is precisely this sort of critical exchange that makes the importation of theory into the classroom a valuable, even essential activity for Ohmann. Teaching for him "is engagement with people other than ourselves, many of whom are open to new (and old) ways of seeing the world." Theory speeds this engagement, by helping to account for the social and economic forces that shape all vision.

In addition to thanking our speakers and respondents, the Center for Literary Studies Committee wishes to thank President Kenneth Ryder, Dean Richard Astro, and those other members of the faculty and staff through whose support and efforts the work of the Center has been accomplished.

Center for Literary Studies Committee

Herbert L. Sussman, Chairperson
Francis C. Blessington
Irene R. Fairley
Jane A. Nelson
Stuart Peterfreund, editor
Kinley E. Roby
Michael Ryan

Christopher Ricks | *Theory and Teaching*

The invitation to speak within this series on "Theory and Teaching" is an honor, and like all honors it carries risks, not least for someone who believes that there are many things even worthier of attention than literary theory. For to decline such an invitation can easily be represented as leaving theory in possession of the entire field of argument, while to accept can equally easily be represented as engaging not only *with* but *in* theory. Better, on balance, to accept, since the latter representation one is present to contest.

Three-quarters of an hour would not be time enough to articulate a cogent theory, but it may be time to enunciate some convictions and to indicate some grounds for them. This will necessarily be open to the objection which the philosopher can always make, that of being "underdescribed" and 'underargued." (The philosopher in turn can often be accused either of overdescription and overargument or of inhabiting a world in which the possibility of overdescription and overargument goes unimagined.)

Against the claims of theory, I set the counterclaims of principle. These may sometimes be counterclaims in the sense that they are at odds with theory's claims, and sometimes in the sense that they put in a competing bid for what will always, in teaching and out of it, be limited resources, notably those severely limited resources time and energy and attention. Very often my beliefs have been best expressed by others; this is for me not an admission but an acknowledgement, since it makes thought about literature continuous with literature, where too I repeatedly find my beliefs best expressed by others.

When Hopkins wrote of the "teachable element" in literature, it was not of theory that he was thinking, and his words may remind us of one continuing alternative claim upon the attentions of teachers and taught, whether in school, college, or graduate school. Hopkins speaks of how poets should learn, and what he says is constant with how we might learn about as well as from poets.

> The strictly poetical insight and inspiration of our poetry seems to me to be of the very finest, finer perhaps than the Greek; but its rhetoric is inadequate—seldom firstrate, mostly only just sufficient, sometimes even below par. By rhetoric I mean all the common and teachable element in literature, what grammar is to speech, what thoroughbass is to music, what theatrical experience gives to playwrights.[1]

Hopkins enunciates a principle; because it is a principle and not a theory he is moved naturally to speak of experience, to which principle, as by definition less comprehensively ideate than theory, gives a correspondingly greater weight. Rhetoric, this teachable element in literature, is not theory, and it still has its legitimate claims and must not be ousted. Rhetoric, granted, is not literature, but that is not because this teachable element departs, rather because something else arrives, a ministering to wisdom, or to justice or to vitality or to magnanimity, such as does not rest content with persuasion. Literature is, among other things, principled rhetoric, and Hopkin's words need to be complemented by T.S. Eliot's, when, embarking upon editorship of *The Criterion*, he spoke of principles:

A literary review should maintain the application, in literature, of principles which have their consequences also in politics and in private conduct.... To maintain the autonomy, and the disinterestedness, of every human activity, and to perceive it in relation to every other, require a considerable discipline. It is the function of a literary review to maintain the autonomy and disinterestedness of literature, and at the same time to exhibit the relations of literature—not to "life," as something contrasted to literature, but to all the other activities, which, together with literature, are the components of life.[2]

Such a sense of literature's relations is itself a statement of principle, and is incompatible with subservience. Literary study, like literature itself, has always needed to resist not only the imperialism of science, which is often frankly adversarial, but also those humanities which are literature's allies but do have their neo-imperialistic ambitions. History, with its insistence that facts are its province, and philosophy, with its confidence that truths are its province: these are often tempted to invade. One of them is always manifestly a greater threat to literature and to literary study than is the other, but therefore not for very long. It used to be history, now it is philosophy. The evidence that literary study is in danger of being philosophized out of autonomous existence is the fact that, as literary theory, it now supposes itself not just able to learn from philosophy (so it should) but able to adjudicate within the discipline of philosophy. John Searle may be wrong and Richard Rorty right, but literary study is vulnerably overextended when (as a discipline, not as individual asseveration) it presumes to rule upon the matter. The world of the philosophers is everything which is their case, and is not our oyster.

This is not to impugn motives; replying to Gerald Graff here at the Center for Literary Studies, Richard Ohmann joined him in deploring any shifting of attention "to the psychopolitical motivations of opposing theorists." But the poisoned atmosphere is now such that each side mutters, of any such disarming plea, "Que messieurs les assassins commencement...." When Christopher Norris (whom I take to be one of the most dedicated and resourceful of literary theory's advocates) applauds Rorty and deplores Searle, not for the homely reason that Rorty at present is, in Norris's judgment, of more use to literary studies, but with the interventionist claim that Rorty is philosophically in the right and Searle in the wrong, he is not so much overweening (his self-delighting word) as underwitting. For to speak of Searle's indictment of Derrida as having "more to do with professional self-esteem than with the interests of reason and truth"[3]; to say that "Territorial imperatives were clearly at stake when John Searle...launch[ed] an attack on this whole new breed of overweening literary theorists"; and to sum it up as "this aggressively self-promoting line": is all this not insouciant (naively so, to use their much-wielded word) about any retort of *tu quoque*? Why isn't the theorist's enterprise equally vulnerable to motive-seeking? Why aren't "professional self-esteem" and "territorial imperatives" and an "aggressively self-promoting line" just as easy to retort upon the literary theorist? It is unlikely that either party has a monopoly of impure motives.

Much of all this is grimly at one with international conflict. Does each side ask only to live and let live? Or does each side maintain both that the other power is an evil encroachment bent upon world-domination, *and* that the others can keep their Mickey Mouse system if they want to?

Resistance to what seem to some of us, or at any rate to me, the inordinate and unspecific claims of theory will sometimes turn upon claims made for it and not just by it. Resistance will often wish to suggest the losses inseparable from a thoroughgoing dedication to theory's comprehensive articulation. Thus one remarkable feature of theory, its impressive intellectuality, is necessarily a limitation too, since there is a difference between intelligence and intellectuality, a difference which has often been the site of valuable disagreements between the English and the French life of the mind. T.S. Eliot wrote in his memorial of John Maynard Keynes (strangely little-known, even to economists):

What one immediately remarked, and most distinctly remembered, about Maynard Keynes, when first meeting him twenty-five or more years ago, was a very exceptional intelligence. The use of "intelligence" here suggests the French, rather than the English associations of the word. That is already, however, making a suggestion which needs at once to be corrected. It is on a somewhat lower level, that of the most alert un-creative mind, that intelligence is a French rather than an English characteristic. When it is united to a powerful and original intellect, it is probably as rare in one race as in another. Certainly, Keynes was quite English, and, in any sense of the word, an "intellectual". That is to say, he was born into, and always lived in, an intellectual environment; he had intellectual tastes; and he had—what is not always denoted by "intellectual"—an intellect. But his mind was also intelligent: it was highly sceptical, and free from the bias of enthusiasm; furthermore, it was a free mind, in that his interests were not limited by the activities in which his talents were supreme.[4]

Behind this there lie both Eliot's disagreement with and his equally substantial agreement with D.H. Lawrence about thinking and intelligence. Intelligence, as both understood and evinced by Lawrence, aspires to be continuous with that which it works upon, whereas intellectuality—with its sense of the advantages to be gained from specialization and its disjunctions—does not. The distinction is not between thinking and feeling, though it may involve very different apprehensions of the duties and priorities within thinking and feeling and the relations between them. Theory, because of its elaborated intellectuality, is not well-adapted to exactly that salience which was seized upon by Eliot (whose philosophical competence was not less than that of his present disparagers, such as Harold Bloom and Geoffrey Hartman) in ending some reflections on contemporary poetry: "intelligence, of which an important function is the discernment of exactly what, and how much, we feel in any given situation."[5] This is one of the great statements of principle not only about intelligence and about literature (since Eliot, like literature itself, is so thoughtful about feeling, and so aware of the difference between the task of combining and the luxury of confusing), but also germane to that more circumscribed essential thing, the profession of teaching. Fortunately we are not obliged to pick only one goal, but if I ever had to, as a classroom teacher, it would not be the fullest possible self-consciousness of methodology and theory, but this principle of

Eliot's: "intelligence, of which an important function is the discernment of exactly what, and how much, we feel in any given situation." I'd select this for, above all, two reasons. First (since literary study should be instinct with social and political judgments), that the world in which we live is still one hideously imperilled by falsity of feeling, so that it is as much a responsibility of the artist and of the teacher to bring people to understand *illusions* of feeling as feelings. Eliot wrote: "Stendhal's scenes, some of them, and some of his phrases, read like cutting one's own throat; they are a terrible humiliation to read, in the understanding of human feelings and human illusions of feeling that they force upon the reader."[6] The sheer *understanding* of this, which everywhere animates Eliot's great poems, has hardly become less needed in a society which is happy that television's Mr. Rogers should educate children into human illusions of feeling. And my second reason for giving such priority to Eliot's insight is that the classroom teacher should maximize the advantages, and minimize the disadvantages, of one crucial respect in which she or he ordinarily differs from the author: that of being physically in the room with those whom one is to reach and teach. To teach the works of Stendhal is very different from reading them. Teaching's humanity must impinge differently—not more powerfully or more honorably but with the continual obligation to confront, even if then to affront, the feelings of those physically present, the obligation of just those living adjustments, allowances, re-adjustments, apprehensions and concessions which it is the glory of Stendhal's art *not* to deal in—not least because Stendhal is no longer alive whereas teacher and taught are hoped to be so. In one elementary sense, the novel says the same to its readers even though it means differently. But the classroom can never afford to be above the suspicion of condescension and of sparing or not sparing people's feelings. ("I am afraid that this is sure to hurt X's feelings," Dr. F. R. Leavis once said of a notorious disciple—"but then he has so many of them.") Intimate with feeling, the intelligence of literature, as of the classroom, is less intellectually ideate than it behooves theory, with its philosophical aspiration, to be.

The point is not any brainless accusation that theory is "cerebral" and lacks feelings; it teems with feelings, but far from being dedicated to "the discernment of exactly what, and how much, we feel in any given situation," theory's advocates often write in such a way as to preclude or occlude exactly such discernment. The banter, untiring and tiring, which plays over titles, for instance, is not in itself evidence for or against the possession of a sense of humor; but it does often ring as an unease uncomprehended, and in particular an unease about the understanding of one's own feelings, within literature and in literary studies. The characteristic titles are not jokes, they are jokey. The current issue of *Critical Inquiry* (September 1984) has an exchange between Edward Pechter and Christine Froula. Pechter's title is: "When Pechter Reads Froula Pretending She's Eve Reading Milton; or, New Feminist is But Old Priest Writ Large." Froula's title is: "Pechter's Spectre: Milton's Bogey Writ Small; or, Why Is He Afraid of Virginia Woolf?" Here are queasy feelings about self-advertisement and self-respect, about literariness and literary studies. The edgy jokiness is a throwing-up of the hands. I don't myself mind being tickled by feather-titles, but I'd rather it weren't at the back of the throat.

It is always a question in these arguments whether to name names. To do so is to risk being, or being accused of being, *ad hominem*; not to do so is to make accusation culpably easy by sousing "on all the kind." My disagreements with, for instance, Frank Kermode do have a personal edge, but they begin in professional opposition. Since he is the foremost advocate of literary theory in— or of—England, it is best to be explicit about what is, on my terms, this one issue. His essay, "Figures in the carpet: on recent theories of narrative discourse," (1980) is the work of a particular man; but the alternative to attending to particular men is attending to straw men. The essay begins:

> It is commonplace that over the past fifteen years or so we have witnessed extraordinary transformations in literary theory and critical method. Those who hoped to keep quiet, sit it out, and wait for a return to normal must now suppose that they have lost their wager. We have without question, had some sort of revolution....[7]

Who are those local losers? Are Donald Davie and William Empson and Hugh Kenner among those who hoped to sit it out but then lost a wager? Is there no such thing as honest opposition either to the claim that there *have* truly been "extraordinary transformations in literary theory and critical method" or to the "transformations" themselves? This travestying of the unnamed opposition is alive with feelings, but the feelings are not there to be contemplated and so they issue naturally, ten lines later, in the concessive climax of Kermode's introductory history of what he himself calls "some sort of revolution": "And by now we may perhaps say that the bandwagon is slowing down a bit; it is easier to climb aboard, or anyway to inspect the goods on offer and make a choice." What ten lines earlier had been "some sort of revolution", has reassuringly, ruefully, become a bandwagon. The bantering demeanor or demeaning banter has its polemical power, but at the price of keeping obscured, from the writer as much as from the reader, exactly what is felt, and how much, in the given situation. The irony is in the service of *"in, but not of"*—but the one thing you can't decently be in but not of is the swim. You can't be both aboard the bandwagon and above it.

The second page of Kermode's review of theories of literature is an act of laudatory non-concurrence.

If one asked what motivated the whole Formalist-Structuralist enterprise, one of the answers (not the only one) would have to be that the wish for something like a science of literature is inveterate. 'In order to become, finally, a science, literary history must lay claim to reliability', said Tynjanov (quoted here) in 1927. Fifty years later his successors are still dreaming of a future in which they will have at their disposal a fully developed scientific method, a usable suprasentential grammar for instance; the present book[8] also dreams such dreams, taking the view that there are no essential differences between the requirements of research in *science de la littérature* and in the physical sciences, or none that will not yield to a version of Popper's falsification procedures. It is not easy to feel confident about these aspirations. 'Any theory of literature should develop methods to guarantee that the observations and conclusions of the scholar are not obstructed by his personal preferences and values. The very first step in that direction depends on the will to avoid such interference by subjective conditions'. To abolish *interest*, to root out *prejudice*: these are noble aims, but they will not be achieved. Still,

> there are some gains by the way:
>> as no chemic yet the elixir got,
>>> But glorifies his pregnant pot,
>>> If by the way to him befall
>> Some odoriferous thing, or medicinal.... [sic]

Kermode does not argue *why* these are noble aims. For me they are not noble at all. The glide from "preferences" to "values" is indifferent to truth and to language, and the easy recourse to the word "subjective," and then to "prejudice," to which "values" become assimilated, is implacably hostile to literature. For the assumption that "personal values" constitute an "interference," like the longing for a "guarantee" that all such interferences would be avoided, entails the extirpation not merely of prejudice but of judgment and therefore of literature. It is the peril of literature, but also its glory, that values, convictions, beliefs and profound enduring agreements constitute not only its nature but its medium, language; such is one reason, admittedly, why literature and language are not enough in this life. Far from its being noble to seek to transform the study of literature into "a science," it is the clerk's highest treason.

> These are noble aims, but they will not be achieved.
> Still, there are some gains by the way:
>> And as no chemic yet the elixir got,
>>> But glorifies his pregnant pot,
>>> If by the way to him befall
>> Some odoriferous thing, or medicinal....

Now what are we to feel (not just think) about these lines of Donne? Do they help us to discern, not only what we think but also what we feel, about these matters of both personal and professional moment? Kermode does not give us the complete first line ("And as no chemic yet the elixir got," instead of "as no chemic..."), and this for the good reason that Donne's "And" would invite the previous line. But is it so easy to issue no invitation to the previous line? "Oh, 'tis imposture all: / And as no chemic yet the elixir got...." Is the reader being tipped a wink ("Oh, 'tis imposture all")? There is no way of knowing, and no way of not wondering. In the very passage in which inappropriate aspirations are prized in the study of literature, an appropriate responsibility is slighted. The quotation from Donne muddies the element, and makes not clearer but obscurer the discernment of exactly what, and how much, is felt. The particular irony is of winks tipped and untipped, but the obstruction of discernment—in this important question of the understanding of feeling—is characteristic of the advocacy of literary theory. The arch charms of Stanley Fish and Geoffrey Hartman are different in timbre but are likewise concerned at once to ease and to obstruct: to ease acquiescence of sentiment and to obstruct discernment of feeling.

The understanding of feeling here has its relation to the understanding of conviction and commitment, and to the continual doubt as to exactly what credit or credence the advocates of theory really place, and invite us to place, either in theory in general or in any one theory in particular. As I heard one of those powerful people say the other day, powerful and (he was insisting) committed, "I'm a post-structuralist, I guess." It has been said of D.H. Lawrence's religion that it is all going to church and never getting there; it may be said of the theory revolution that it is all marching to the barricades and never getting there. Here I stand, I can no other, I guess. The thin cry, "I'm not saying that I agree with it..." rises so often that I for one value more than ever those critics who urge writings, whether primary or secondary, upon us because they *do* believe in them—critics like Leavis, Empson, Winters, Trilling, or—from an adjacent discipline—Christopher Hill.

The diffused complaint that theory is not taken seriously is attuned to the largest claim of theory, one which is essentially a claim *to* and not a claim *that*: specifically, a claim to the utmost attention. Insofar as the large claim is made accessible to specific dissent, it turns upon indispensability. The question becomes not legitimate self-defense, whether theorists may do as they choose, but the claim enshrined in "indispensable" that everybody must do as theorists choose; that is, engage with and in theory. And "must" is then polemically compounded of two very different things, the one a bolthole when there is trouble for the other: "must" as "are inevitably involved in theorizing whether or not they know it and admit it," and "must" as "really ought to face up to their professional obligations." In his recent advocacy of theory, Christopher Norris says of William Ray's book *Literary Meaning: From Phenomenology to Deconstruction* that much of its "great virtue" is its "refusing to let go of the idea that theory—intelligent theory, if you like—is indispensably a part of the reader's role." "'Intelligent theory', if you like": well, even I prefer it, but yet may not like the move that suddenly calls it up. Still, the claim itself is clear: theory is indispensably a part of the reader's role. Not desirable, not even very desirable, but indispensable. But the longing for something indispensable, for a *sine qua non*, is part of the long history of being misguided not only about literary studies but about literature itself. Theory as "indispensably a part of the reader's role": but *indispensable* when used like this is a blank check (like the undiscriminated invoking of "relevance"). Indispensable in what way to the reader's role exactly? If in every way, the assertion is preposterous; if not in every way, then how? Later in Norris's essay the claim looks as if it is being made more specific, when Norris concurs with J. M. Bernstein's *The Philosophy of the Novel*: "Theory is indispensably the precondition of enlightened modern thinking, strive as it may to recapture the innocence of communal narrative forms." But could there not be such a thing as unenlightened or non-enlightened modern thinking? Or does self-appointed enlightment now enjoy a monopoly of thinking? (The theorist's attack on social complacency is itself then breathtakingly complacent.)

Much of the covert action within such a claim is effected, as so often, by recourse to the myth of the Fall: "to recapture the innocence of communal narrative forms"; or again, "post-structuralism has altered our habits of thought beyond hope of a return to the innocence of unreflective origins." With the same appeal to the same myth, Kermode could say in 1970: "I had been writing criticism for years without bothering too much about how I did it, but I now find that I am increasingly absorbed with theoretical issues, and foresee no possible reversion to a state of innocence."[9] In 1984 S. S. Prawer can say: "though she once mentions Propp... Ms. Shaw situates her criticism in a garden of pre-structuralist and pre-deconstructionist innocence."[10]

Now reports of the innocence of critics prior to the "revolution," critics such as Coleridge or Eliot or Empson or Trilling, have been much exaggerated, like reports of the death of the author or of God. But the more immediate matter is this indispensable invoking of the Fall. It is manifestly *the* myth or metaphor with which to seek to rebuke the gullibility of any attempt to put the clock back (a metaphor which is itself often gullibly used, since it is not true that you can't put the clock back, and we regularly and rationally do it for travel or for daylight saving). But even if we were to accept the loaded metaphor of the Fall, is it loaded exactly as "enlightened modern thinking" would wish? For there is something itself "unreflective," and "naive," and insufficiently de-constructive about this marked refusal then to interrogate the Fall. For the Fall is not the story of pure gains, but of great gains and great losses. Even by the most hopeful interpretation of the *felix culpa*, fallen man does not enjoy all conceivable felicity. To take seriously the invoking of the Fall (which means not permitting its merely threatening use) is at once to be moved to consider the very matter which the advocates of theory least wish to be raised: that of the losses inseparable from ours being the age, not of (in Prawer's words) "a garden of pre-structuralist and pre-deconstructionist innocence," but of structuralist and deconstructionist—what? nocence? The loss of innocence must entail not only experience but also nocence, harmfulness. If Prawer and the others wish to invoke Eden's innocence, let them meet their self-chosen obligation to think about their metaphor, and not only to concede but to consider what has been lost and the new harm done. Milton says of the snake, still innocent, "Nor nocent yet...."

The advocates of theory often declare that we are all theorists whether we realize it and acknowledge it or not. This stratagem has its risks, notably that of eviscerating not just your opponent's argument but the entire argument itself. Of course the declaration can be made invulnerable, by the simple expedient of so defining theory. Coleridge said, "To think at all is to theorize."[11] But the trouble with Coleridge's provocation is that there is then, as so often, a need for another word, to make the still-necessary distinction between what used to be called theory and other kinds of thinking. Gerald Graff concedes too much when he says *theory* "in the sense of a descriptive analysis of the nature of literature," as if any degree of such descriptive analysis constituted theory. There is a political oppression in this refusal to admit an alternative, as there is in the politician's phrase which has gained Mrs. Thatcher the acronym-nickname Tina—There Is No Alternative.

It is a great convenience to maintain or pretend that there is no distinction between thinking at all and theorizing, but it does itself incur its inconvenience. In *Criticism in the Wilderness* Geoffrey Hartman says: "Leavis's refusal to acknowledge that he was a theoretician *malgré lui* showed how strongly fixed the aversion to theorizing had become"; "There were English stirrings of theory, nevertheless: in Richards's work especially, even if 'principles' sounded more modest and practicable than laws, methods, etc."[12] But this is the convenience of misrepresentation. Hartman gives no evidence at all that Leavis was refusing to acknowledge something. This is insulting not only to Leavis but also to René Wellek, since the famous exchange in *Scrutiny* between Leavis and Wellek, on the value or indispensability of philosophy and theory in the study of literature, was believed by both Leavis and Wellek to be a substantive disagreement. The adjudication of the dispute in Wellek's favor (as English criticism mostly has not adjudicated it) would be one thing; but the unargued dissolving of the dispute into a spectral combat between a theoretician and a theoretician *malgré lui* is an act of condescension. Since Hartman refuses to acknowledge that there are such things as principles and that they differ from theory (and not only from "laws, methods, etc."), he feels himself under no obligation even to imagine what might count as evidence for his assertion against Leavis. The tactic, throughout Hartman's book, is to divide all criticism into two camps: theory, and practical criticism. If it is acknowledged, just for once, that someone used the word "principles," he is merely being English and sly, and availing himself of the fact that the word "principles" sounds modest and practicable. But the strength, say, of William Empson's criticism is always its commitment to principles and not to theory, and this strength is clear in one of his apophthegms, itself a principle about principles: "Life involves maintaining oneself between contradictions which can't be solved by analysis" (Note to "Bacchus"). It is in philosophy that something is *stigmatized* as a paradox.

Yet the alternative exists, and a dedication not to literary theory but to literary principles is neither a self-deception (Hartman's Leavis) nor a subterfuge (Hartman's young Richards) but a grounded choice. Theory, if the word is to be required to continue to mean—as it should—something both more and less than thinking, is characterized by its degree of elaboration, concatenation, completeness, abstraction, self-consciousness, explicitness, regression, recession and technicality. None of these is unique to theory, and since matters of degree are involved, there will always be disputed instances. But to deny that theory is characterized by something—indeed, by some such things—is simply not to win but to nullify the argument. The word "theory" points towards philosophy, which is why Hartman can speak repeatedly of "theoretical or philosophical criticism," and of the "philosophy of theory." It would be as debilitating to claim that all men who think are philosophers as it would be to claim that there is on every occasion a clear-cut distinction of kind. T.S. Eliot, who could have held down a job in the philosophy department of Harvard but fortunately found even better things to do, at once made a concession to theory and was more or less sceptical of it: "While we may of course, and must in fact, make theories more or less, explain our feelings to ourselves and others: still our theories are, like Mr. Santayana's 'consciousness,' only a phosphorescence." One distinction for Eliot turned on the difference between evading and avoiding: "To communicate impressions is difficult; to communicate a co-ordinated system of impressions is more difficult; to theorize demands vast ingenuity, and to avoid theorizing requires vast honesty."[13] The work of Fish and Hartman and Culler demands vast ingenuity, and they impressively meet this demand; but ingenuity is not only not all, it is not—as the relative lightness of the word itself allows—one of the very highest values either in literature or in the study of literature.

In his vast honesty, Dr. Johnson stands as the greatest of English critics, and his greatness is not distinct from his sustained and rational opposition to philosophy and to theory. "The task of criticism" was, for Johnson, to "establish principles" (*Rambler* No. 92), and he everywhere made clear that his refusal to elaborate and concatenate the needed concepts beyond a certain point (a point reached early) was not a refusal to continue to think, but a decision to think thereafter about the application of the principles rather than to elaborate principle into theory.

A fully-fledged theory, taking wing, is a philosophy; a fully compacted principle is rooted as a proverb. Theory is necessarily, and for its purposes honorably, hostile to contradictions; proverbs admit contradictions, and leave us to think not about that but about applicability; we are to decide which of two contradictory truths ("Look before you leap" / "He who hesitates is lost," or "Absence makes the heart grow fonder" / "Out of sight, out of mind") applies in any given situation. Eliot's use of those last words—"intelligence, of which an important function is the discernment of exactly what, and how much, we feel in any given situation"—points to his here involving not theory but a principle; for theory, by reason of its proper, if then paradoxically limited, ambitions, seeks exactly to generalize and not to be circumscribed by "any given situation." One cannot but be in two minds about Blake's notorious generalization that "to generalize is to be an idiot," but to generalize is to enter into a new circumscription. Principles, like proverbs, suppose that difficulties are as much worth our attention as are problems; theory, like philosophy, is committed to pressing that once you have said (as Raymond Williams has about these issues) "What you must do is to admit that a problem exists," you have an obligation to attend to the problem. But what is the nature of the obligation, especially in relation to other obligations? Of course there are theoretical, philosophical, problems about literature; about what are there not? Aggressive advocates of theory are like mountaineering missionary extremists who would claim, not just that they may climb Everest because it is there, or even that they must climb it because it is there, but that we must all climb Everest because it is there.

The antagonism of theory to principles turns on the value and priority of a high degree of elaborated and regressive concatenation. But theorists themselves necessarily do not *complete* elaboration or regression; they too, quite properly except for their often averting their eyes from it, arbitrate a point "thus far and no further." For once you insist on regressive or recessive elaborations, not one of your own terms is stable. The death of D.H. Lawrence in 1930 moved E.M. Forster "to say straight out that he was the greatest imaginative novelist of our generation." Whereupon T.S. Eliot's recessive philosophical proclivities, which he usually resisted when writing literature or about literature, notoriously encouraged him to speak in the wrong regressive way: "The virtue of speaking out is somewhat diminished if what one speaks is not sense. And unless we know exactly what Mr. Forster means by *greatest, imaginative* and *novelist*, I submit that this judgement is meaningless." But the philosophical incitement was disabling, not enabling, and Forster did well to resist it and to turn the tables on it: "Mr. T.S. Eliot duly entangles me in his web. He asks what exactly I mean by 'greatest,' 'imaginative' and 'novelist', and I cannot say. Worse still, I cannot even say what 'exactly' means—only that there are occasions when I would rather feel like a fly than a spider, and that the death of D.H. Lawrence is one of these."[14] For the resistance to the philosophical web was no less dextrous than powerful. Eliot's "exactly" is just as open to retort as Forster's "greatest." Those who stall or forestall the reading of a poem by first asking combatively what it is to *read* can themselves be asked the prior question of what it is to *to*. The existence of a problem need entail no obligation to grapple with it. Every page of literary theory, as of every other discourse, is for instance involved with the question of whether there is freedom of the will, a question that is of course tacitly set aside.

Hartman says that "the most peculiar feature of philosophical criticism is indeed the difficult alliance in it between speculation and close reading."[15] But why is not other literary criticism, non-philosophical criticism, equally characterized by the "difficult alliance in it between speculation and close reading"? The implication that philosophical criticism has a monopoly of speculation or of the difficult alliance will not bear either speculation or close reading. For such non-philosophical critics as Donald Davie are engaged in speculation and in close reading and in the difficult alliance of the two. For me, the most peculiar feature of Hartman's philosophical criticism is its claiming that the difficult alliance between speculation and close reading is a peculiar feature of philosphical criticism. It is a short step from the risky handy proposition that to think at all is to theorize, to the oppositely risky handy one that only theorists think at all. At this point, admittedly, my resistance to such claims for theory moves into resentment. Hartman again: "The resistance to theory in Anglo-American criticism goes together with a resistance to imported ideas, from non-English countries or from other fields of inquiry, the social sciences, in particular."[16] But such pre-revolutionary and anti-revolutionary critics, resistant to theory, as Eliot, Trilling, Kenner and Davie can responsibly be accused of resistance neither to imported ideas from non-English countries nor to imported ideas from other fields of inquiry. Their criticism repeatedly has recourse to both. More modestly, or more immodestly, at any rate more personally, I resent the assertion that resistance to theory "goes together with" such resistances. When ten years ago I wrote a book on Keats and embarrassment, the enterprise in my judgment did not have to welcome literary theory, but it was more than happy to welcome "other fields of inquiry, the social sciences, in particular"— Charles Darwin on *The Expression of the Emotions in Man and Animals* and Erving Goffman and others on embarrassment and blushing socially and biologically considered. But once again the advocates of theory will have their other weapon at the ready, prepared if it comes to it, to baptize with a hose; I was not surprised, during the Cambridge rows which were either about the worth of structuralism or about the worth of Colin MacCabe, to be told by *The Guardian* newspaper that *Keats and Embarrassment* was a structuralist book. "A theoretician *malgré lui*"; a structuralist *malgré lui*. But if I am *le médecin malgré lui*, the opponent is Tartuffe.

Principles permit of counter-principles, as proverbs do. A theory, because its reputability is constituted of elaborated concatenation, does not permit of a counter-theory. It claims a much higher degree of comprehensiveness and of sustained cogency ("philosophy or theory"), and it therefore asks to be taken as a whole. There would be something odd about *not* believing both proverb-principles "Look before you leap" and "He who hesitates is lost." Granted, both theories and principles are subscribed to, but the cost of the subscription to a theory is very high, and almost all such subscriptions lapse.

Instances of principles matter because of the instances which the principles would themselves illuminate and be illuminated by. Eliot makes a point of principle when he says of wit that "it involves, probably, a recognition, implicit in the expression of every experience, of other kinds of experience that are possible" ("Andrew Marvell"). This is profound in its economical exactitude, and in the application which Eliot makes of it to metaphysical poetry, and in the living possibilities of further imaginative application which it fecundates. No doubt a theory could be elaborated to accommodate Eliot's principle here; but why exactly should it be? Or why should mustering such a theoretical elaboration have top or high priority? To do this is to not to do that. The claims of the applied and experiential are not *prima facie* less worthy than the claims of the generalized and the ideate.

The question is not whether, say, a Wayne C. Booth should be discouraged from theoretical elaborations of irony, but whether William Empson should be stigmatized as innocent, naive, unreflective, and so on, when he does not elaborate such flexibly suggestive formulations of principle as his saying that "An irony has no point unless it is true, in some degree, in both senses; for it is imagined as part of an argument; what is said is made absurd, but it is what the opponent might say."[17] I find this a more persuasive and a more clarificatory way of conceiving of irony—and especially of distinguishing it from its malignant sibling, sarcasm—than is available to me in the more theoretically comprehensive accounts of the matter. It is Empson's principle of irony ("true, in some degree, in both senses") which helps me to understand the force, for instance, of D.J. Enright's poem "Streets":

STREETS

The poem was entitled "The Streets of Hanoi,"
It told of falling bombs and death and destruction
And misery and pain and wastage.
The poem was set to music, which told of death
And destruction and misery and pain and wastage

A hall was found to play it in, a singer to sing it,
An orchestra to accompany the singer, and a printer
To print the programme... Whereupon it was felt
(Things being what they happened to be) that
The song had better be called "The Streets of Saigon."

It was well sung, well played, and well received.

Truly poetry is international, just like music,
And falling bombs and death and destruction
And misery and pain and wastage,

Truly we only need one poet in the world
Since local references can be inserted by editors,
Theatre managers or clerks in the Culture Ministries.[18]

Indignation is always tempted by sarcasm, but Enright achieves
the more magnanimous (and therefore *more* telling) thing, irony.
For the axis upon which this fine political poem turns, the line
which it is itself obliged to live up to, is one which would be
misheard if it were heard as sarcasm: "Truly poetry is international,
just like music." "True, in some degree, in both senses": truly (and
not just with sorrowful headshaking at the preposterousness of
such a thought) poetry *is* international, but not in the easy empty
way which would suffocate political conscience—such as is true
here and now—under the pseudo-transcendental verities (for
Hanoi, read Saigon). Enright's poem validates Empson's principle,
and *vice versa*; the principle itself resists ease though it facilitates
both understanding and application. Empson himself pointed out
that Pope's great couplet "Now Lapdogs give themselves the
rowzing Shake, / And Sleepless Lovers, just at Twelve, awake,"
gains its power (as irony, *not* sarcasm, which is inferior in its

superiority) from the fact that though the couplet is not credulous about whether "Sleepless" lovers are really to be believed, it is true to some degree in both senses: for to have been sleepless all night, tossing and turning, is often to fall into a drugged sleep at dawn from which you may wake only at noon. The reader who is awake to Pope's width of mind, at once magnanimous and shrewd, will value Empson's principle and Empson's instance, and will not be obliged to wish that Empson, instead of doing this, had done the other thing, of constituting a theory of the matter. I say "instead" because it is one ground, for resistance to theory's insistences, that the advocates of theory sound as if no sacrifices ever had to be made, as if all of us could and should do all. Had we but world enough and time.... Teachers have particular responsibility to consider "world enough and time," because the time that they most spend is not their own.

Hopkins, who was a great critic, pre-eminently in his letters, set down an unforgettable and endlessly applicable principle in his unfolding of Tennyson and "Parnassian." Hopkin's letter to A.W.M. Baillie moves with beautiful pertinence:

Sept. 10, 1864.

Dear Baillie,

Your letter has been sent to me from Hampstead. It has just come, and I do a rare thing with me, begin at once on an answer. I have just finished *The Philippics* of Cicero and an hour remains before bedtime; no one except Wharton would begin a new book at that time of night, so I was reading *Henry IV*, when your letter was brought in—a great enjoyment.

The letter-writer on principle does not make his letter only an *answer*; it is a work embodying perhaps answers to questions put by his correspondent but that is not its main motive. Therefore it is as a rule not well to write with a received letter fresh on you. I suppose the right way is to let it sink into you, and reply after a day or two. I do not know why I have said all this.

Do you know, a horrible thing has happened to me. I have begun to *doubt* Tennyson. (Baillejus ap. Hopk.) It is a great *argumentum*, a great clue, that our minds jump together even if it be a leap into the dark. I cannot tell you how amused and I must say pleased and comforted by this coincidence I am.[19]

From reading Cicero and *Henry IV*, to reading a letter, to thinking about the principles of writing a letter ("The letter-writer on principle does not make his letter only an *answer*"), to thinking about those principles of poetry and of "poetical criticism" which are to be the letter's enterprise: the modulation and momentum are superb, and so is Hopkins finding appropriate amusement, pleasure and comfort in his being so in sympathy with Baillie about this new qualifying of his sympathy with Tennyson.

Hopkins's letter, famous and inexhaustible, sets out the principles which distinguish "the language of inspiration" from "Parnassian," which "can only be spoken by poets, but is not in the highest sense poetry." The movement of Hopkins's mind is as naturally a move from a principle to an instance as then from instance back to principle—but never into theory.

> Great men, poets I mean, have each their own dialect as it were of Parnassian, formed generally as they go on writing, and at last,—this is the point to marked,—they can see things in this Parnassian way and describe them in this Parnassian tongue, without further effort of inspiration. In a poet's particular kind of Parnassian lies most of his style, of his manner, of his mannerism if you like. But I must not go farther without giving you instances of Parnassian. I shall take one from Tennyson, and from *Enoch Arden*,[20] from a passage much quoted already and which will be no doubt often quoted, the description of Enoch's tropical island.
>
> > The mountain wooded to the peak, the lawns
> > And winding glades high up like ways to Heaven,
> > The slender coco's drooping crown of plumes,
> > The lightning flash of insect and of bird,
> > The lustre of the long convolvuluses
> > That coil'd around the stately stems, and ran
> > Ev'n to the limit of the land, the glows
> > And glories of the broad belt of the world,
> > All these he saw.
>
> Now it is a mark of Parnassian that one could conceive oneself writing it if one were the poet. Do not say that *if* you were Shakespeare you can imagine yourself writing Hamlet, because that is just what I think you can*not* conceive.

What makes this statement of principle, with its persuasive instance, so thrilling is its own inspiration, especially in that last leap.

> Now it is a mark of Parnassian that one could conceive oneself writing it if one were the poet. Do not say that *if* you were Shakespeare you can imagine yourself writing Hamlet, because that is just what I think you can*not* conceive.

For it is a mark of Hopkins's genius that though I could, I suppose, conceive of myself coming up with, or coming down to, some distinction between the inspired and the not inspired, I cannot conceive of myself creating the penetrating terms of this principle itself: "Now it is a mark of Parnassian that one could conceive oneself writing it if one were the poet." More, Hopkins's critical feat at once goes beyond critical Parnassianism; do not say that *if* you were Hopkins you can imagine yourself writing these sentences, because that is just what I think you can*not* conceive. Inspiration there is perfectly at one with courtesy, as it was in the opening of this immediately-answering letter, when Hopkins, "on principle," goes into a letter's needing to be more than an answer; the courtesy within the astonishing, and immediately convincing, appeal to Shakespeare and *Hamlet* is manifest in the sequence, "because that is just what I think you can*not* conceive." Not "just what you can*not* conceive," but "just what I think you can*not* conceive." This is the perfection of two kinds of consideration, the co-operation of a considered principle with a considerate tact. Principle and tact are as intimately co-operative in criticism as are comparison and analysis; and it can be a grounded objection to theory that its being reasoned is on occasion no compensation for its being tactless.

Richard Ohmann, with characteristic candor, has said, again here at the Center for Literary Studies: "I am suggesting that maybe we could profitably, we the people who talk about this kind of thing at all, spend our time better by concentrating on the concept of literature, rather than on literature." My priorities are obviously the opposite; I cannot conceive of spending my time better than on literature, and, in particular, particular works. If, say, a great song of Bob Dylan's is not literature, that is only because its medium is not words alone. I take "One Too Many Mornings" to be a work of art, the hearing of which should be welcome.

ONE TOO MANY MORNINGS

Down the street the dogs are barkin'
And the day is a-gettin' dark
As the night comes in a-fallin'
The dogs'll lose their bark
An' the silent night will shatter
From the sounds inside my mind
For I'm one too many mornings
And a thousand miles behind.

From the crossroads of my doorstep
My eyes they start to fade
As I turn my head back to the room
Where my love and I have laid
An' I gaze back to the street
The sidewalk and the sign
And I'm one too many mornings
An' a thousand miles behind.

It's a restless hungry feeling
That don't mean no one no good
When ev'rything I'm a-sayin'
You can say it just as good
You're right from your side
I'm right from mine
We're both just one too many mornings
An' a thousand miles behind.[21]

Randall Jarrell defined a novel as a prose fiction of a certain length with something wrong with it. Had I but world enough and time, I should wish to bring out that principles, unlike theories, are keen to engage in discriminating, and to apply Hopkins's principle, with patience, so as to understand just what goes wrong and why, throughout the middle stanza of this lovely song. "From the crossroads of my doorstep / My eyes they start to fade...." This, unlike the first and last stanzas which are inspired, is Parnassian, and—like most Parnassian—it is, in its complaisance, vulnerable to humor, such a worse than unwanted suggestion as "From the crossroads of my doorstep / My eyes they start to cross." I can conceive myself writing "the crossroads of my doorstep" if I were Dylan—and I do not say to myself that if I were Dylan I can imagine myself writing the inspired no-rhyme of "good" and "good" in the song's last stanza, at once the fullest and most conclusive rhyme of all (the word itself repeated) and the emptiest and least of rhymes at just the point where the previous stanzas have fully clinched their rhymes:

> It's a restless hungry feeling
> That don't mean no one no good
> When ev'rything I'm a-sayin'
> You can say it just as good....

This, in its pained numbness, is something quite other than "From the crossroads of my doorstep," which I can conceive myself writing if I were the artist who wrote, elsewhere, "through the smoke rings of my mind." Do not say that *if* you were Shakespeare you can imagine yourself writing *Hamlet*; come to that, do not say that *if* you were Dylan you can imagine yourself writing "Ophelia, she's 'neath the window, / For her I feel so afraid...." The point is not that Hopkins's principle is conclusive, as theory not only may but in some respects must seek to be, but that such a principle is inaugurative, and when invoked leaves much still to say.

The claim for principles, as against theory, involves both senses of the word *application*. Another matter, equally intimate with teaching, is that of discontinuity and continuity, since the intense specialization that is consummated theory is necessarily, and not idly, the acceptance of a series of substantial discontinuities where principles seek to maintain or effect continuities. For the thoroughly systematic nature of theory induces that dislocation of which Kierkegaard said: "In relation to their systems most systematizers are like a man who builds an enormous castle and lives in a shack close by; they do not live in their own enormous systematic buildings." (The authors of books which argue that books are written by their readers still expect to draw royalties; and others who disclaim the invoking of intentions claim that their intentions have been misrepresented.) System and theory are not that by which men live or even really try to live; sometimes this makes for the comedy of hypocrisy, and always it makes against that continuity which Eliot incarnated in the word "principles": "A literary review should maintain the application, in literature, of principles which have their consequences also in politics and in private conduct."

Theory, in its professionalized and systematic intellectuality, widens the gap between critics and non-professional readers; between critics and writers; between critics and scholars; and—smaller of scale but professionally germane—between graduates and undergraduates. Hartman, for whom the *only* alternative to theory is "practical criticism," says roundly that "practical criticism is more of a pedagogical and propaedeutic than mature activity" (the word "propaedeutic" itself being intended to cow the young and immature); he speaks then of "the mind of the novice," and of "the danger in this undergraduate or undeveloped form of practical criticism."[22] I share none of the beliefs which underlie such a way of speaking, such an estimate of practical criticism in any of its forms, or of undergraduates, or of the alternatives as Hartman conceives them. But I am sure that Hartman is right to depict theory, or advanced thought as they like to think it, as intrinsically inimical to undergraduate teaching. Kermode is reported (in *New Society*) to have said that "the real work for undergraduates should be on a pre-theoretical level" (the conceded existence of such a level itself coming as quite a surprise, but the implications of "pre-theoretical" as against "non-theoretical" being no surprise); when Kermode announced that he found himself "increasingly absorbed with theoretical issues," it was natural to move, two sentences later, to saying: "I think one ought sometimes to write deliberately for audiences which include laymen and students, but I do it less than before." "Include," not consist of, "laymen and students...."

But when time is almost up, it is time to stress once more that theory and teaching do not have all the time in the world. Several great critics have been educators, but only one great critic devoted his professional lifetime to the profound inspection of education.

He is regularly disparaged these days as having both practiced and incited a resistance to theory, but the resistance itself is related in Matthew Arnold to a deep understanding of one crucial principle in teaching and especially in the teaching of literature. Presenting a selection from the great criticism of his great predecessor Johnson, *The Lives of the Poets*, Matthew Arnold deplored "the common notion" that education is advanced "by for ever adding fresh matters of instruction." Arnold instead offered at the start of his preface the essential educative principle of the limits within which education, like life itself, needs to acknowledge that it lives:

> Life is short, and our faculties of attention and of recollection are limited; in education we proceed as if our life were endless, and our powers of attention and recollection inexhaustible. We have not time or strength to deal with half of the matters which are thrown upon our minds, they prove a useless load to us. When some one talked to Themistocles of an art of memory, he answered: "Teach me rather to forget!"

Notes

1. 7 August 1886; *The Correspondence of G.M. Hopkins and R.W. Dixon*, ed. C.C. Abbott (1935; 1955), p. 141.

2. *The Criterion*, i (1923), 421.

3. *London Review of Books*, 2 August-6 September 1984.

4. *New English Weekly*, 16 May 1946.

5. *The Egoist*, iv (1917), 151.

6. *The Athenaeum*, 30 May 1919.

7. *Comparative Criticism Yearbook*, ii (1980), 291.

8. Fokkema and Kunne-Ibsch, *Theories of Literature in the Twentieth Century*.

9. *New American Review*, ix (1970), 82.

10. *Times Literary Supplement*, 17 August 1984.

11. *The Friend*, Section the First, Essay iv; ed. Barbara E. Rooke (1975), i 189. I owe this to Luther Tyler's witty review of Jerome Christensen; *South Carolina Review*, xvi (1983), 126.

12. (1980), p. 7. Some paragraphs in what follows derive from a piece of mine in the *London Review of Books*, 16 April-6 May 1981.

13. *The Athenaeum*, 27 June 1919.

14. *Nation and Athenaeum*, 29 March, 5 April, and 12 April 1930.

15. *Criticism in the Wilderness*, p. 174.

16. p. 297.

17. *Some Versions of Pastoral* (1935), p. 56.

18. *New York Review of Books*, 13 August 1970. Reprinted by permission of Mr. Enright.

19. *Further Letters of G.M. Hopkins*, ed. C.C. Abbott (1938; 1956), p. 215ff.

20. Published that year.

21. © 1964, 1966, Warner Bros. Inc. All Rights Reserved. Used By Permission.

22. pp. 296, 298.

Stephen Owen | Response

It is instructive as well as disquieting to observe how the acceptance of a particular role forces us toward a predetermined relation, and from that relation, into a position. I was astonished to observe my own reaction to Mr. Ricks' paper: despite my public professions of dissatisfaction with what has been done to literary theory in recent years, I felt here a powerful urge to rush to the defense of that diverse aggregate of activities which claim, collectively, to *be* literary theory. Mr. Ricks' paper is a principled opposition to the claims of theory; and my initial reaction to such opposition teaches me to be wary of adversarial rituals by which one tacitly accepts an "opponent's" definition of the boundaries of dispute.

I prefer to break the rhythms of conflict to consider the traditions which inform the conflict and its dangerous consequences. To put it succinctly, to accept this particular conflict is to lose. To accept the conflict is to grant that the claims made for theory or the advocacy of theory or writing *about* theory are in the same category as writing literary theory (a much rarer enterprise). Second, to accept the conflict is to grant that problems inherent in the writing of theory are more significant that the internal values of the activity; i.e. whether it is done well or poorly.

When we reflect on the conflict as it is given to us, I would encourage that we acknowledge the force of historical traditions in literary study, which are as powerful as traditions in literature itself. Within Anglo-American literary study there has been a recurrent motif of enthusiastic advocacy of continental theory, met and opposed by an evolving notion of purely English values: plain and concrete language, a terse refusal to elaborate, and the role of literature in a moral education. An early example occurs in Dryden, who has Neander judiciously moderate Lisideius' adoration of French dramatic theory. Later, Coleridge's often vacuous Teutonizing was met with sensible scorn. Sometimes talent lies on one side of the conflict; sometimes on the other. But in this tradition it is the *advocacy* of theory, rather than theory itself, which plays the role in the historical game.

Despite the claims of both "theory" and "principle" to eternal and international validity, literary study is bound to a particular history. There are distinct modes of writing on literature in Germany, and somewhat different ones in France, each with its own history and its own accepted relation to its national literature. We allow that such distinctions are both valid and real, but quickly grow uncomfortable when it is pointed out that we inhabit one of those local histories. The Anglo-American tradition lives by rhythms of conflict: on the one hand, claims for the embarrassing superiority of continental theory (usually accompanied by the assumption that no one in the purely English tradition can think—an assumption eagerly ratified by French and German exporters); on the other hand, a defense of "native" traditions and a general distrust of anything that resembles continental theory. Mr. Ricks is well aware of this history and consciously takes a stand on one side of the conflict. I note that every critic Mr. Ricks cites with approval is English, or in a few cases, American. I note also that when he speaks of maintaining the barriers between literature and philosophy, it is the highly professionalized tradition of English philosophy to which he refers. There are other traditions of philosophy in which the boundaries between philosophy, literature, and writing on literature are more open. And beyond the modern continental traditions, there is the classicist, who moves comfortably between Thucydides, Plato, and the dramatists without the least anxiety that literature is endangered by the neighboring domains of history and philosophy.

Still more remarkable, in the continental traditions a criticism of "principle" exists side by side with literary theory, with little sense of irreconcilable conflict between the two. Few German theorists would disdain to take one of Goethe's comments on literature seriously; in contrast, the Anglo-American advocates of theory often seem embarrassed to consider a statement by Dr. Johnson as anything more than a symptom of a given age or literary tradition.

It is an odd circumstance, this local tradition of mutual contempt between the advocate of theory and the critic of principle. I confess that I have been unable to discover any substantial grounds for the *conflict*. Substantial *differences* exist, but these are generic. Earlier I spoke of the dangers of accepting the conflict: the received structure of conflict forces an individual to oppose and to discover reasons for opposing what one would otherwise not oppose. Even worse, the boundaries drawn in the historical conflict force alliances and confusions across truly substantial divisions.

Mr. Ricks delivers a fiercely cogent attack against the aberrant claims made regarding theory, but he goes on to attack theory itself. In doing so he points up quite well how the nature of theoretical endeavor tends to generate just such excessive claims. But in discovering reasons for his opposition—even good reasons, I believe—he is a victim of this historical structure of conflict. Let me descend to those simple and reasonable truths we are usually embarrassed to mention. Even though theory, in one of its most characteristic western forms, may aspire to terminate further discussion, it never has done so and it never can. Literary theory is essentially a delightful and harmless activity which, in the past two millennia, has produced some excellent—occasionally, indispensable—books, which live side by side with other kinds of writing on literature. One may prefer it or not; but even if one does not prefer it, one nevertheless should allow that the activity of theory has produced some books which, if unread, will leave students the poorer. Aristotle's *Poetics* involves "elaboration, concatenation, completeness, abstraction, self-consciousness, regression, recession, and technicality." Mr. Ricks and I would both reject the transformation of this book into a pedagogic tyranny—it *has* happened, several times. Yet, even though such a transformation may appear to be warranted by certain internal claims of the *Poetics*, most of us would agree that such misuse does not constitute grounds to reject the *Poetics* as a work not worthy taking seriously. Older literary theory is a valuable reminder that we can take such a work seriously without accepting its claims to command belief and be the "last word." Perhaps the crucial point is the question, which is "literary theory": Aristotle's *Poetics*, or a pedagogy that propounds the *Poetics* as an authorized orthodox paradigm for understanding literature?

I suspect that I could go on and get Mr. Ricks to agree that a work like Schiller's "Naive and Sentimental Poetry" is valuable in the same way that the *Poetics* is valuable. But now I will cross a boundary of sorts and suggest that, were it not for Derrida's Anglo-American advocates, Mr. Ricks might find similar interest and value in Derrida writing on *Phaedrus*. Unfortunately this is a moot supposition because at present Derrida cannot be cleanly extricated from the conflict in its present round—indeed, he participates in it.

Let us, once and for all, distinguish the *writing* of literary theory from the *advocacy* of theory's virtues, the *production* of epitomes of other people's thought, and the *appeal* for collective allegiance. Good theoretical writing is an art of thought, with its own pleasures—different in kind, but not necessarily in degree, from the pleasures of reading Dr. Johnson. Theory is something which is done in the *particular*; and though it sometimes aspires to voiceless universality, it is successful only when it embodies a *particular* voice and turn of mind. Theorizing is an activity, but the only valid model of the activity is offered by particular books and particular essays: theory cannot properly be the common property of a sect. Such books can be very important in the study and teaching of literature, but their importance depends upon an obliquity—they are books we have read which return to us by chance when we read and reflect on literature. A good example of such a work deserves to be taken seriously, and we may discover that we believe part or all of it (as is the case with Mr. Ricks' description of principle, we may discover that we believe contradictory works of this sort); nevertheless, such a work should not *command* belief. I think we can understand these proper values of theory by remembering older works which have outlived sectarian conflict.

The sectarian rituals of Anglo-American literary study transform this proper role of theory into something else. We should wonder what happens here—why an interesting activity, supported by a long tradition of valuable books, suddenly becomes strident cant. Anglo-American folkways, exacerbated by the demands of academic pedagogy, strip the activity of its individual voice, mechanize it, and strangest of all, make it a badge of status and value. Suddenly it commands communal belief. We cannot ignore here the needs of a corrupt pedagogy, asking some recognizable mastery of technique as a proof of education, and combining that with structures of progress, in which the techniques of production must be regularly improved and supplanted. In this model of literary education as heavy industry, theory is distinctly "white collar."

Many of the things Mr. Ricks objects to in the advocacy of theory are nothing more than the symptoms of this metamorphosis: pride in having modernized the factory of the mind, a compulsion which disdains particular products (the processing of poems), and the graded progressivity of literary education, involving mastery of ever more difficult techniques. I would share with Mr. Ricks the desire to rescue literary education from this; however, I suppose I part company from Mr. Ricks in desiring also to rescue literary theory from this.

If we face the situation honestly, I think we will discover that teaching is the nexus of the problem, rather than some secondary activity which passively bears the consequences of the problem. In academic literary education powerful social mechanisms are already in place, mechanisms which have their own inertia and to which we feel a powerful pressure to conform. To oppose the motions of those mechanisms is to risk scorn and incomprehension; and for student or younger faculty, opposition is to risk more serious consequences that follow from the disapproval of one's teachers or colleagues.

Literary theory has been transformed into a packaged guarantee of understanding; claims of its indispensability and perfect teachability smell of the qualification procedures of a guild. The force of these guild-needs is such that it can assimilate even theoretical texts which convincingly undermine the grounds for such use. The ironies in this process are painful: I recall one of those numerous recent epitomes of deconstruction which hierarchically grades various theorists on how radically they undermine the project of hierarchical grading.

I understand Mr. Ricks quite clearly. I am not trying to claim that he is a theorist in spite of himself. His paper really does oppose the genuine theoretical impulse, together with those other activities that masquerade as literary theory. But I think he has taken some of the Anglo-American advocates of theory at their word and has treated distinct activities as though they were one. I do not doubt the sincerity of his convictions, but I must express the suspicion that in a different climate conviction would be rather preference and disposition. As distinct dispositions of thought rather than as opposing camps in a conflict, "principle" and "theory" form an interesting pair. They are, in a sense, contradictory truths; and I wholeheartedly agree with Mr. Ricks in valuing contradictory truths to which we can simultaneously subscribe.

If there must be conflict, let the common enemy be the academic domestication of either disposition; and let the common goal be a thoughtful teaching which outwits the drive to guild formation.

Robert Scholes | Interpretation and Criticism in the Classroom

You invited me to speak to you on "the influence of developments in semiotics on the teaching of literature." This proposal, which I have carefully quoted verbatim from Kinley Roby's letter to me of 21 February 1984, is, like any other statement of consequence, in need of interpretation. We might ask, for instance, whether this "influence" I am supposed to discuss should be regarded as something that *has* happened, *is* happening, or *may or may not* happen. We might also consider whether or not the proposal implied that I should argue on behalf of the influence of semiotics upon the teaching of literature; that is, argue that this influence is or would be a good thing. One might, in fact, have a happy old interpretive time with this brief text from Roby, advancing and rejecting various positions, considering the text's presuppositions, its intertexts, its contexts, its position in Roby's epistolary oeuvre, and so on.

Attractive as it appears to be, we are not going to embark on this course, for reasons I shall be explaining. But first we must pause to consider one false reason for rejecting this direction of inquiry. If I actually undertook the project of making Roby's text the focus of our critical attention, some practical soul would be certain to ask why I couldn't have just called him up and *asked* what he meant by "the influence of developments in semiotics on teaching." Why not, indeed? I could have called—it's true—but I couldn't *just* have called. I am not a person who *just* calls. Anyone. Ever. That's how I am. For further details I refer interested parties to Roland Barthes's discussion of telephoning in *A Lover's Discourse*. And by way of support for my action—that is, my action in *not* calling in this particular instance—I can say that Roby gave us no indication of a desire to be called, or even a willingness to be called. His letter, for instance, included no phone number. The absence of a sign may be itself a sign. But that is not why I didn't call. I didn't call because (a) anything Roby told me would still have to be interpreted, and (b) I thought I understood the message well enough in the first place. I took the message to mean: "Say something about the way semiotics—for which you are perceived as an advocate or spokesperson—can actually improve our teaching of literature." Understanding Roby's message in that sense, in accepting his invitation I had made a commitment that any good speech-act philosopher could analyze in considerable detail. Personally, I understood my commitment as involving acceptance of the proposition that I could indeed speak *for* semiotics, advocating some semiotic approach to the teaching of literary texts. And this is precisely what I intend to do—but with certain reservations that I must make clear at the outset.

First of all, I think we must resist our American tendency to package and commodify every idea, attitude or approach and market it as a nostrum. I have been guilty of this in the past—and perhaps will be again—but I am trying to resist this powerful cultural pressure as strongly as I can, and as steadily as I can. I do not, in fact, have a product called "semiotics" to sell. For me "semiotics" has come to be the name for the problems I am interested in, rather than for any set of solutions to these problems that I might offer. In thirty years of teaching English my sense of the fundamental problems and goals of the discipline has shifted from concern with teaching a set of literary works to concern for the development of certain textual skills in my students: skills that are demonstrated in the making of new texts and in responding to old ones. These activities of encoding and decoding texts I now perceive as semiotic activities. That is, I see the object of study—the thing that students need to master in order to improve their ability to read and write—I see the object of study as certain culturally determined structures of discourse—sometimes called "codes"— that mediate the production and reception of texts.

In speaking of a shift in the object of my activities as an English teacher, I do not mean to suggest some unique personal discovery on my part. I think the whole profession has been experiencing this shift, though different individuals have interpreted it in different ways. For me personally, certain studies in structuralist and post-structuralist theory have led to a particular way of naming and describing my new orientation. Calling it "semiotic" is simply my way of taming it, of trying to obtain textual power over it—which is what naming is all about. Along with the name "semiotics," of course, come new objects of study and new methods of studying. The most important of these, as I have already indicated, are discursive formations or codes.

To focus on codes (in the sense developed by Roland Barthes) or structures of discourse (in the sense developed by Michel Foucault) is to identify an object of study that has more in common with traditional studies of rhetoric than with the recent history of literary interpretation. Such an approach broadens the field of possible texts for study to include all types of expository, persuasive, and documentary discourses, and it shifts attention from the individual work and the author to the cultural structures in which both are embedded. This is not just another way of teaching literature; it is a way of teaching something else: a something else in which literary works may be included, but without their old privileges.

I have suggested that we are experiencing a shift in the discipline of English—a shift which is itself a symptom of larger cultural changes. This shift can be described as a swing of the pendulum that seems to govern the relative emphasis on rhetoric and poetics in the institutionalized study of language and literature over the centuries. Or it can be seen as a change to something quite new, involving new technologies, new media, and a new cultural situation. However one describes it, the change is real enough to exert pressure upon our academic lives. I personally believe that we have some freedom in our response to such changes. They affect us but they do not, I believe, totally determine us. Specifically, we may choose to adopt the semiotic response to this situation, or we may dig in and try to hold the line on behalf of traditional literary values. I understand that reactionary impulse, and sometimes feel it myself, though on the whole I am of the other persuasion. On this occasion I shall try to clarify what is at stake in choosing between these two views, by pointing out some of the ideological implications of adopting one or the other. Traditional literary instruction has as its goal the development of a particular skill of great importance: *interpretation*. Interpretation, as it has been taught in our literature departments for some decades, stresses what Paul Ricoeur has called the "positive hermeneutic." That is, interpretation teaches a submissive approach to the deep or hidden meanings of texts that have already, in advance, been accorded the privileged status of scripture or (what is almost the same thing) of literature. Interpretation assumes the permanence of truth, including truths about human nature. It is essentially and inevitably a conservative and even reactionary process.

On the other hand, rhetorical and semiotic instruction have as their goal the development of a different but equally important skill: *criticism*, which is based upon what Ricoeur calls a "negative hermeneutic." This skill has been neglected in our literature classrooms for reasons that are now perfectly obvious. The great privilege accorded the literary text in our dominant modes of study has made any criticism of such texts seem an impertinence. The "New Criticism," for instance, was really not a mode of criticism but of interpretation. Its critical judgments were made in advance, at the level of selection of texts, and all that was left was explication and interpretation. The semiotic approach requires a democratization of the canon, a de-privileging of the protected and sacred texts—a world in which all texts are open to criticism. To the semiotician, literary texts are especially powerful instances of the operation of cultural hegemony. They are the vehicles through which ideologies are disseminated and sustained: powerful and subtle engines of propaganda. All of which means that the place of literature in the curriculum is not simply being challenged. There is no point in throwing out Milton and bringing in the Rolling Stones or Dr. P. Joseph Goebbels. The point is to study all the vehicles of cultural manipulation—or a rich and varied sample of them—with a critical eye.

I have sketched very briefly here the position developed at some length in my recent study, *Textual Power*. In that book I have elaborated on the notions of "interpretation" and "criticism" that I am employing here, and I have attempted (in Chapters 2, 3, and 4) to demonstrate their implications for teaching through discussions of short narratives by Ernest Hemingway. The present essay is intended as an extension of those three chapters and their predecessor, "Decoding Papa," in my earlier book, *Semiotics and Interpretation*. I mention these previous studies because—though I have tried to make this essay intelligible by itself—my pedagogic stance is largely worked out in them, the present essay being intended as an extension of a position already developed elsewhere. What I propose to do here is to illustrate some ways in which Hemingway can be used in the sort of textual pedagogy that I am advocating. We can begin with some lines from his story "Cat in the Rain." They appear in the first paragraph of the story, which is a description of the setting: an Italian resort.

> It was raining. The rain dripped from the palm trees. Water stood in pools on the gravel paths. The sea broke in a long line in the rain and slipped back down the beach to come up and break again in a long line in the rain.

There are three elements or phases possible in textual response. The first is simply *reading*: getting the message, reaching the bottom line. This text is odd, however, in that the bottom line comes first. Actually, it is not so odd. The formula of a general statement followed by illustration is a familiar one. It is especially familiar to readers of newspapers. First the headlines and the important information, then details of an increasingly trivial sort—since readers are lost with each new paragraph. Ernest Hemingway, as he has explained in *Death in the Afternoon*, was a journalist trying to become a literary artist. The whole process can be observed in these few sentences. The "headline"—"It was raining"—in this case is followed by purely descriptive details of a striking redundancy. If it is raining, of course rain will drip from the palm trees. ("It's gotta go somewhere.") Mere *reading*, as we may think of it, is troubled by the redundancy in texts of this sort. It is this "trouble" that drives us to either drop the text or advance to another level of response. What can't be read must be interpreted. Even an excess of simple repetition can drive us to seek the non-simple, the hidden meaning, and to perceive the text as a work of "literature."

Thus, we move to *interpretation*. Interpretation calls upon all texts to stand and yield their hidden meanings. As every high school person understands, *interpretation* is what the teacher knows and you don't—("so shut up and learn something, dummy!") Interpretation was made for the secretive text, the consequential text, the sacred, legal, or literary text. While the mere reader is stuck on denotation ("So it was raining, so what?"), the interpreter sees the connotative level and rejoices. What is rain but an endless repetition of the same? Every snowflake may be unique, a little individual, but all raindrops are alike, an endless horde of sameness. ("And what does the sea have in common with rain, class?" "They're both made of water." "Yes, but...someone else?" "The waves of the sea repeat one another like the raindrops, so that the combination of waves and rain produces a double connotation of monotony." "That is correct.")

A double connotation of monotony! It is true, of course, and this is indeed a basic procedure of verbal art: the clustering of connotations around a matrix that is itself unnamed. The word "monotony" does not appear but the concept is generated connotatively. It is a skill that should be learned, and students should learn not only to decode in this way but to encode as well. Still, there is more in the text. Consider the last sentence again: "The sea broke in a long line in the rain and slipped back down the beach to come up and break again in a long line in the rain." The repetition of prepositional phrases linking the waves and the rain—"in a long line in the rain"—both governed by the identical preposition (as alike as two raindrops) also connotes monotony and connotes it doubly because the whole phrase is repeated. Hemingway does not say that the waves kept breaking. He describes them breaking *and breaking* in exactly the same words. The last clause of the sentence—"and slipped back down the beach to come up and break again in a long line in the rain"—could be repeated infinitely without damaging the syntax of the sentence. Like the waves, the sentence breaks, dwindles into prepositional phrases, threatening to match the waves in its remorseless redundancy.

It all adds to the connotations of monotony, of course, but it also carries meaning in another code. These words are saying: "Look at us. We are functioning in an art sentence. We are only little words, such as anyone might use, but our Papa has arranged us so cunningly that we have become an exemplary bit of modernist prose. File us with Flaubert, Conrad, and Joyce." The sentence, in other words, connotes monotony, on the one hand (or in one code), and art—especially modernist art—on the other. This is not a sin. Most artists are show-offs, as a stroll through any gallery will reveal. (Why does Vermeer, for instance, in his *Mistress and Maid*, have to paint the light hitting a clear glass and a tiny carafe with a spherical stopper?) Hemingway is asserting himself as an artist in these sentences, and this is just as much one of the text's meanings as is the connotation of monotony or the denotation of rain. His whole career shift, from journalist to artist, is mirrored in this prose.

These few sentences, however, monotonously interesting as they are, will not afford us sufficient scope to get much beyond interpretation in the direction of criticism, but we can take a tentative step or two in that direction. Those sentences ask for recognition as art of a particular sort—modernist prose—a prose very different from that of the great Victorians or their predecessors. This prose is connected not only to Flaubert but to Gertrude Stein, and to the verse of Pound and Williams. We are dealing with a period style here as well as a personal one, and our evaluation of such writing will inevitably have something to do with the degree of our commitment to—or appreciation of—the writing that period. But let us move to a larger text that offers more scope for criticism. At this point I must ask you to read Hemingway's story, "Mr, and Mrs. Elliot," from *In Our Time* (Scribners, p. 85).

Criticism, as I have been defining it here, means moving beyond reading and interpretation. In particular, it means discovering the codes that are invoked by a text and exposing the means by which the text seeks to control our responses to it. I have chosen this particular text because it is a witty, satirical piece, and therefore especially dependent upon cultural norms and sanctions. In considering it, I will draw particular attention to the manipulative devices present in the text. We can begin at the beginning: "Mr. and Mrs. Elliot tried very hard to have a baby." Is there anything funny about that? We hear all the time about people who are "trying to have babies," and our response is usually sympathetic. But how often do we hear about people trying *hard* to have babies? Trying *very* hard? I would suggest that there is a hint of the ludicrous even in this first sentence. It is implied by the extent of effort being employed—all great efforts have an element of the ludicrous at least potentially in them—and, of course, by other elements that emerge more clearly with the second sentence: "They tried as often as Mrs. Elliot could stand it."

The idea of trying to have a baby is a vague and spacious notion that covers everything from sperm counts and aphrodisiacs to labor in childbirth. In his second sentence Hemingway has reduced this great matter to one feature: copulation. "Trying to have a baby" means the act of sex, which is supposed to be the most pleasurable physical experience that most of us will ever know. But in these two sentences the act of love-making is described as hard labor, especially for the woman. The pangs of childbirth have been displaced forward to the moment of conception—or rather to the attempt to conceive. In addition to this displacement of the woman's pain, by reducing the idea of trying to the act itself, Hemingway is able to quantify the number of attempts. Normally, if we learn that our friends are trying to have a baby, we do not ask how many times they have tried. By starting a chronicle of trials—"They tried in Boston...and they tried...on the boat" Hemingway presents this honeymoon as a *via dolorosa* with a station of suffering for each new try in each new place.

The humor here, such as it is, is based upon a binary opposition deeply embedded in American culture: the opposition between Puritan and Libertine. In this instance the opposition takes the form of sex as sensual pleasure versus sex as procreative duty. In the liberated 1920's Hemingway is confident that his audience will share his perception that sex as a duty and burden must be ridiculous. The basic Puritan/Libertine opposition is invoked in other instances as well. A particularly telling passage is the description of Hubert Elliott's pre-marital experience:

> He was twenty-five years old and had never gone to bed with a woman until he married Mrs. Elliot. He wanted to keep himself pure so that he could bring to his wife the same purity of mind and body that he expected of her. He called it to himself living straight. He had been in love with various girls before he kissed Mrs. Elliot and always told them sooner or later that he had led a clean life. Nearly all the girls lost interest in him.
> (paragraph 3)

The explicitly puritanical character of Hubert's values is emphasized by the words "pure" and "purity." In the narrative the code of purity is presented as absurd for the very good reason that "girls" are not interested in "men" who lack sexual experience. The American girl, in the view of Hemingway's text, far from being the virtuous, high-minded creature of sentimental literature, is a practical, sensual person, who is simply not interested in male purity.

The episode could easily be translated into the language of advertising. "A recent survey shows that nearly all red-blooded American girls prefer experienced men." Which reminds us that Hemingway has indeed turned his prose to the uses of Madison Avenue. In 1952 his picture and a signed letter graced advertisements for Ballantine Ale. Among other things, he said, "You have to work hard to deserve to drink it. But I would rather have a bottle of Ballantine Ale than any other drink after fighting a really big fish. When something has been taken out of you by strenuous exercise Ballantine puts it back in...." In the ad, Hemingway pushes the ale as a replacement for whatever a man loses while fighting "a really big fish"—some precious bodily fluid, no doubt. At any rate, it is clear that both the ad and the short story rely on a similar male bonding between writer and readers, and a similar authoritative omniscience. Ernest knows what men want—and what women want, too. "Nearly all the girls" want experienced lovers. To the extent that we share the joke on the puritanical Hubert we accept complicity in Hemingway's view. We share his code.

There is something else in the passage, however, that strikes an eye sensitized by contemporary codes of sexual experience. If we edit out Hubert Elliot's puritanism, we get an interesting expression of the *structure* of his attitude toward women, as opposed to the merely sexual content of this instance of that attitude: "He wanted to... bring to his wife the same [condition] of mind and body that he expected of her." An interesting attitude, isn't it: a more genuinely fair and egalitarian attitude toward a woman than we can find in most of the male characters or narrators of Hemingway's *In Our Time*. What I am suggesting is that a *critical* examination of this passage—as opposed to an *interpretation* of it—would have to take account of the text's potential complicity with advertising, its knowing, almost leering assurance about understanding what women really want, and its rejection of the concept of sexual equality that is implicit in Elliot's approach to marriage. To the extent that we accept and enjoy the malicious wit of Hemingway's narration of this incident, we are accepting complicity in, and are being conditioned to, the codes invoked by the text. And the only remedy is the exposure and discussion of those codes.

The sexual code (to which we shall be returning) is traversed in this story by several others that structure the flow of values and pleasure for the reader of the text. One of these codes has to do with writing itself, for Hubert Elliot is a writer: "a poet with an income of nearly ten thousand dollars a year." The bland delivery of these two facts in the same clause forces the reader instantly to the level of interpretation. Why are they mentioned together? What have poetry and money to do with one another? No interpretation without a code! In this case the code seems to be based on a bohemian and romantic notion that the rich are not only barred from the Kingdom of Heaven but from the Province of Poetry as well. In this case, we are also in the presence of a more private and personal code. Hemingway's ambivalent attitude toward the rich (he despised them for corrupting him but allowed it to happen) is well documented. There *were* poets with incomes in Hemingway's Paris (Harry Crosby, for instance). The whole passage constitutes a break in the text, through which personal attitudes may be seen flowing. The money and poetry connection occurs again, however, in paragraph 12, in which we learn that "Hubie," with enough poems for a book, has "sent his check to, and made a contract with, a publisher." Instead of being paid by a publisher for his work, Elliot is paying a publisher to put his work in print. This is called, technically, vanity publication, and, in Hemingway's code, it is a violation of the ethics of writing. Deep beneath this implied contrast between Hubert Elliot, the rich Boston poet who can publish himself, and Ernest Hemingway, the poor midwestern prose writer who must struggle for publication, is the Puritan/Libertine opposition again—only this time Ernest is the Puritan and Hubert the Libertine. This implied contrast between Elliot and himself is also visible in the kind of writing that Elliot does: "He wrote very long poems very rapidly."

Whenever Ernest says "very," watch out! Here he says it twice. Elliot's poems are *very* long and are written *very* rapidly. In the modernist aesthetic, ease and rapidity are the antithesis of quality. We can trace this attitude from the letters of Flaubert and Conrad down through Woolf, Joyce, and Hemingway himself. The idea of poetry being written rapidly—and of very long poems being written very rapidly—was clearly anathema to Hemingway. They *have* to be bad poems in the code that governs this story. Vanity publication only sets the seal on their badness, a badness which is powerfully underlined by the implied contrast with Hemingway himself. Hubert Elliot is the very antithesis of Ernest Hemingway. (Even their initials are reversed: E. H. / H. E.) Hubert writes long poetic texts rapidly; Ernest writes short prose texts slowly.

Meanwhile, the grim pursuit of babyhood continues: "They tried to have a baby in Paris...and they tried several times to have a baby before they left Dijon." And in Touraine "they tried very hard to have a baby in the big hot bedroom on the big, hard bed. Mrs. Elliot was learning the touch system...." The touch system, of course, refers to Mrs. Elliot's typing of the "very long poems," but we are not thinking about typing when that clause opens the sentence after the "big, hard bed." Something odd is going on in this story with respect to sex, and there is a lot of semantic seepage between the sexual and the other topics that the text presents.

One of the prominent features of this text is its reliance on euphemism and innuendo. We have already noticed how the act of copulation is most frequently designated by the formula: "They tried to have a baby." Conversely, the expression "making love" (in paragraph 2), which could easily be an explicit reference to copulation, means in its context only courting or wooing. We know this because we are told explicitly (in paragraph 3) that Elliot "had never gone to bed with a woman until he married Mrs. Elliot." The phrase "gone to bed with" is, of course, the standard euphemism for copulation. Hemingway uses it here so that there can be no mistake about the actual extent of Elliot's sexual experience, but it will reverberate strangely in this text when Cornelia (Mrs. Elliot) and her "girl friend" begin going to bed together at the end of the story.

The only explicit detail of the period during which Elliot was "making love" to Cornelia is that of Elliot's special method of kissing. The text is not explicit enough to tell us what this method involves: we are expected to fill that in from our own sexual encyclopedias. But the text is wonderfully explicit in telling us how Elliot achieved this erotic breakthrough: "He learned that way of kissing from hearing a fellow tell a story once" (paragraph 6). This is both funny and pathetic. What kind of person learns such elementary things from stories? Life imitates art here in the most absurd way. Of course, Cornelia herself is erotically titillated by Hubert's tale of his own innocence: "Sometimes when they had been kissing together a long time, Cornelia would ask him to tell her again that he had kept himself really straight for her. The declaration always set her off again" (paragraph 6). It is not exactly clear what "set her off again" means, but it seems to include what more recent discourse would encode as "turned her on again." Hubert's "declaration" of innocence apparently has an aphrodisiac effect—but it is not the only strange aphrodisiac in the story.

On the wedding night we find Hemingway at his nastiest—and funniest. One rather suspects that he finds the idea of sex in Boston amusing in itself, but he obviously does not rely on all of his readers to share that perception. Paragraph 8 tells the story:

> They spent the night of the day they were married in a Boston hotel. They were both disappointed but finally Cornelia went to sleep. Hubert could not sleep and several times went out and walked up and down the corridor of the hotel in his new Jaeger bathrobe that he had bought for his wedding trip. As he walked he saw all the pairs of shoes, small shoes and big shoes, outside the doors of the hotel rooms. This set his heart to pounding and he hurried back to his own room but Cornelia was asleep. He did not like to waken her and soon everything was quite all right and he slept peacefully.

Their "disappointment" is presented as something so predictable as to need no discussion. Obviously his inexperience might account for this, but the story as a whole suggests another explanation, to which we shall attend in due course. For the moment let us follow Hubert on his nocturnal excursion.

Prowling the corridor in his Jaeger (or huntsman's) bathrobe he encounters the shoes: "all the pairs of shoes, small shoes and big shoes, outside the doors of the hotel rooms." To interpret this, one needs to know the code that once obtained in hotels, whereby the customers' shoes were left outside each door to be polished overnight. In this case, however, a second code is also required. The big shoes and small shoes together suggest couples, coupling in those rooms. But the erotic effect of these shoes also suggests, in a Freudian code, a strange and fetishistic element in Hubert's sexual make-up. At any rate, the shoes "set his heart to pounding." May I ask how you interpret this? I believe that we are in the domain of the sly or nasty euphemism here, in which the heart acts as a metonymic substitute for a more pertinent organ. So the hunter (in his Jaeger) rushes back to undo the disappointment of this wedding night— "but Cornelia was asleep." Another disappointment. However, "soon everything was quite all right."

The interpretive question that must be raised here is *how* did everything become all right. This is one of those places where the reader must, in the phrase of Umberto Eco, write a little "ghost chapter." Hemingway's text is exerting pressure upon us to account for Hubert's peaceful sleep. To my way of thinking the very peacefulness of this sleep combined with the speed ("soon") of Hubert's relief forces us to write our ghost chapter in a particular way. We must masturbate Hubert, and we may well feel resentful at Ernest for requiring us to do it. Otherwise Hubert's rapid lapse into peaceful slumber remains a mystery—and interpretation hates mysteries. I would suggest that it is thematically necessary for us to supply masturbation at this point for another reason. In the last paragraph of the story we find Elliot sleeping alone but looking very exhausted in the morning. One could easily write a ghost chapter that explains this phenomenon, but Hemingway has provided his own narrative in this instance, explaining that Hubert "wrote a great deal of poetry during the night and in the morning looked very exhausted." These nocturnal emissions of poetry, with their exhausting effect on the author, force upon the interpreter an equation of masturbation and versification. Elliot's poetry is presented by Hemingway as verbal self-indulgence and verbal self-abuse. He too, perhaps, has learned "the touch system."

Cornelia, on the other hand, has never really mastered typing. "The girl friend" takes care of that. Just what else she takes care of is also the interpreter's concern. Not to be too coy about this, I would argue that the text strongly suggests that Cornelia's inability to enjoy sex with Hubert is grounded in the fact that her sexual preferences run the other way. Cornelia and her nameless girl friend both come from "very old Southern families," which

Hemingway clearly codes as equivalent to disintegration and decadence: "Like all Southern women Mrs. Elliot disintegrated very quickly" (paragraph 1). Her girl friend calls her "Honey," which is innocent enough, and they have "many good cries together." How innocent is that? The girl friend had been "in" Cornelia's tea shop in Boston, but her capacity there is never clarified by the text. She was "in the front of the shop" the day Hubert first kissed Cornelia in the back, and Cornelia is miserable from the moment she leaves that shop until she prevails upon Hubert to "send over to Boston for her girl friend who had been in the tea shop" (paragraph 11).

Elliot sends and the girl friend comes: "Mrs. Elliot became much brighter after her girl friend came and they had many good cries together" (paragraph 11). Why should having many good cries together make Mrs. Elliot much brighter? Possibly this is a simple matter of companionship, which is reason enough for a person's brightening in this world. But it is also possible that "having a good cry" is another one of those expressions of displaced sexuality that seem to haunt this text. The last paragraph is helpful here: "Mrs. Elliot and the girl friend now slept together in the big mediaeval bed. They had many a good cry together." They are living in a château, with room for many guests. There is no shortage of beds. But Cornelia and her girl friend are sleeping together in the same bed that used to be the scene of those fruitless attempts to have a baby. Now it is apparently the scene of good cries that leave the criers bright and cheerful. In the end they are all "happy": Elliot with his wine, his nocturnal effusions of poetry, and his exhaustion, and Mrs. Elliot with her girl friend as a bed partner, their good cries, and their conversation under the plane tree.

Hemingway obviously took a lot of pleasure in presenting this picture of a rich poet who has to pay for his publication and support the female lover of a wife who has exiled him from the marital bed. If we share in this satirical pleasure, we must do so by accepting these values. We must agree that it is demeaning to have to finance one's own publication and that it is humiliating for a man to be supplanted in bed by a woman. We must, in fact, see the relationship between the two women as degrading for all concerned. One could rewrite this text, however, without too much difficulty, as a truly happy narrative in which two lesbians and an autoerotic shoe-fetishist work out a *modus vivendi* under rather difficult circumstances. Change the hot evening wind to a cool one, provide some critical acclaim for the poems and some less exhaustive recreation for Hubert—and perhaps the château country would seem less like Kansas to all concerned. We might not reach the Land of Oz, of course, but we wouldn't be in a Hemingway hell anymore, either.

Taking a critical attitude toward a story like this involves locating the codes invoked by the text and consciously questioning the extent to which we ought to accept such codes. Do we want to accept the views of Bostonians, Southern women, Harvard law students, homosexuals, girls, literature, and so on proffered by this text? To the extent that we wish to resist any of these views we shall have to refuse the pleasure of the text in order to contest its textual power over us. This is precisely the gesture we are never allowed to make under the regime of interpretation. If we are to encourage our students to move beyond interpretation to criticism, we must see that the Hemingway of the Ballantine Ale advertisement and the Hemingway of the stories are in exactly the same complicity with culture and must be scrutinized with the same critical eye.

It should be obvious from the example we have just considered that such a move toward criticism does not imply a rejection of interpretation. Far from it. We have needed interpretation every step of the way. The question, as I see it, is not that of a choice between interpretation and criticism but of a choice between accepting interpretation as the end of textual response or positioning it as the means to an end which is truly critical. There can be no criticism without interpretation, but it is fatally easy to interpret without taking a critical position. My whole discussion here has been an attempt to illustrate both how and why teachers should help their students to become not just interpreters but critics as well.

Susan R. Horton | *Response*

I didn't have Professor Scholes' paper in advance. But if one believes, along with Lacan, that all speech is heard as a response to the *hearer's* desires anyway, then it follows that there can never be "adequation" between a given speech and the pre-existent desire in the hearer who regards it as a response. Acting on the basis of what I wished to hear, I anticipated the talk I desired Professor Scholes to give—one which would, of course, be good but not quite adequate. Having now heard his paper, I still believe my assumptions, anticipation, and response to be essentially correct.

He and I are on the same side. I have also argued in favor of demystifying things for students, whether that means pointing out those codes by which we read and through which we see the world, or whether in composition classes that means refusing to teach grammar, or the "rules" of the game, without telling students what the game is: what discourse is, and what kinds generate and represent what kinds of power. Not telling students the real nature of our enterprise preserves hegemonies; keeps insiders in, and outsiders out. Worse, our recent mystifications, specifically post-structuralist theories, have generated for our profession the same risk Egyptian priests faced: we've created a hieroglyphics so few can read only a new Rosetta stone may prevent our texts from becoming entirely unreadable. Awareness of these twin dangers accounts, I think, both for the current anti-theory rumblings in surprising places, and for our renewed interest in explaining to students what it is we really *do* when we read and interpret literature.

Professor Scholes has worked for years to do this, warning us about the dangers of mystification and the dangers, as well, of imposing arbitrary ways of seeing on students. For instance, in his recent *College English* essay, "Is There a Fish in This Text?" he shrewdly points out that the old story about Louis Agassiz, the great teacher who finally got his students to "really *see*" the fish in front of them, really teaches us something quite different from what we thought. Agassiz's student, Scholes rightly points out, learned to "see" the fish not by looking at it, but by going home and thinking about what Agassiz *wanted* him to see: to see in ways *he* had privileged. I want to argue today that Professor Scholes' reading of Hemingway's "Mr. and Mrs. Elliot," which purports simply to teach students by way of the codes to see what is *in* that story, in fact and despite Scholes' best intentions, is another version of the same fish story.

In my brief discussion, I do not want to respond to or challenge much his reading of "Mr. and Mrs. Elliot." Instead, I want to address and answer the two very efficacious questions behind all of his writings, including "Is There a Fish in This Text," and his *Semiotics and Interpretation*. In both places, he asks two questions: "What, if anything, have we learned about textual interpretation that has direct implications for pedagogical practice," and "What specific interpretive attitudes and strategies that are currently active offer us the best models?"

What I want to argue is that Professor Scholes' questions are exactly the right ones, but that he has not yet realized how far his own questions might take us towards creating the more humane and open pedagogy I know he advocates. If we ask his two questions with post-structuralist theory in mind, we will stop far short of what we might discover if we assume that what we should do is *teach* those theories in the classroom. Properly construed, deconstruction is not a method at all, but a set of awarenesses and a stance of self-critical questioning.

In what I believe to be the true deconstructive spirit, then, and in response both to today's paper and to Christopher Ricks's earlier offering in this series, I want to suggest that those of us who argue *for* the importation of theory into the classroom and those of us who argue *against* the importation of theory into the classroom are arguing those positions while standing on precisely the same ground, and while failing to question that ground. Both positions assume the same relation of teacher to student: teacher as one who is distanced, objective, holding no relation to students but that of disseminator, determinor of what shall and shall not be poured into them. That view of the student / teacher relation is evident in Professor Scholes' language today, and especially in the earlier chapters of *Semiotics and Interpretation*: "Students *need*...." "The student...*must be exposed*...." "The teacher *transmits*...." In this model, which both pro-theorite and anti-theorite share, the student is all permeable membrane; the teacher, all impermeable membrane. One need only turn those formulations on their heads: "What does the *teacher* need?" "To what must the *teacher* be exposed?" "What does the *student* transmit?" to realize not only how foreign they sound, but how liberating consideration of those questions might be.

The central question of Derridean deconstruction is "What does writing write?" Its focus is on "the *scene* of writing." To import theory into the classroom should not mean only or necessarily that we teach students to become adept at answering that particular deconstructive question, although surely we might want to do that. What is important, it seems to me, is that this particular deconstructive question *not* be allowed to harden into a hypostasis radically opposite to its spirit. If we only ask "What does writing write?" in the classroom, we ensure the post-structuralist legacy will be nothing but one more method to add to the arsenal of interpretive strategies we teach, and deconstruction itself will be seen, and rightly, as nothing more than what Paul deMan called "a passing squall in the intellectual weather." The transformed and transformative focus I'd like to see Professor Scholes and all of us have is a focus on not just the scene of writing, but on *the scene of teaching*. And our central deconstructive question is not "Should we teach the codes," or "How should we teach the codes," but instead, *"What does teaching the codes teach?"*

Despite his insistence that we make students aware of the principle *scribo, ergo sum*—I produce texts, therefore I am—Professor Scholes and all the rest of us have stopped short of the next step: a recognition that the *classroom* is also a text, produced by teacher and student in collaboration. There is a semiotics of *that* text, too, and it is time we studied it, exactly as Scholes himself has studied the semiotics of the text that was the collaboration of Louis Agassiz and his students learning to "see" the fish.

In Professor Scholes' reading of "Mr. and Mrs. Elliot," for instance, I am surprised that what to me are the most obvious operative codes are not even mentioned. In the story's opening we have an unhappy woman looking increasingly older than her years trying valiantly to conceive Mr. Elliot's baby and type his poems. By story's end, we have a woman sleeping with a woman friend, and "waking up cheerful." Whatever codes Professor Scholes sees in the story seem to me to pale before the obvious one: we have here a tale of Sisterhood. Professor Scholes' intricate wonderings about what the two women *do* in bed, exactly, will itself be a code all women will recognize with some bemusement. Now the point is not that there are "conflicting codes" in the story, and not that the teacher has access to the "right" codes, and has an obligation to disseminate those to the students because they "need" them. If in fact the codes are encoding the wisdom of the culture, and if the student is a part of that culture, presumably the student comes to the classroom with a rather extensive set of encodings fully in place. While the teacher seems to be revealing only what's "there" in the story, my example of rival but suppressed codes suggests something far more interesting to consider here.

At the scene of teaching, we have two human beings, each with a set of encodings fully in place. Each is able to recognize and identify a "code" because it has in some way been a part of his or her experience. But the one member of this pair, the teacher, has the power and authority to take what he identified from his experience, training, tradition, and project that experience or habitual way of seeing back into the text, thus turning the personal into the "universal," and announcing that he has identified a "code" at work in the text. The student, unless he or she be particularly brave, finds his or her codes unnamed, unrecognized: not privileged. So one answer to my earlier inverted question, "What does the teacher need or get from teaching," now comes into view. In teaching the codes, the teacher gets a great deal back: identification of himself with a hegemony and a habitual way of seeing, recruitment of new members to the way of seeing, and a suppression of alternative ways of encoding.

The lateness and reluctance with which we come to begin to study what our teaching teaches seems to me in uncanny ways to prove the Freudian and Lacanian assertion that ignorance is active: a refusal of information. There are thousands of books on what to teach, but precious few really about pedagogy, or exploring what our teaching really teaches. There were those quiet (in the event) books by Ohmann, Ellmann, Poirier. There is Friere now; there are a few others. So far, post-structuralist theorists have been as evasive as everyone else. The Yale French Studies volume *The Pedagogical Imperative*, with a few notable exceptions, does what Professor Scholes does here. Barbara Johnson talks about pedagogy there by analyzing Moliere's "L'Ecole des femmes." When we finally get around to analyzing a classroom, why must it be a *literary* classroom? Why do we talk about what texts we should teach, ignoring the one text we must *all* teach: our own action in the classroom. Why do we "dance around the circle and suppose," to quote Frost, when "the secret sits in the center, and knows."

I want to suggest that our willed blind spot is the direct consequence of our reluctance to confront our ambivalence about our relationship to students, and to teaching. Behind the debate— and more importantly behind the *vehemence* of the debate—over whether theory should or shouldn't be imported into the classroom, for instance, is a hidden ambivalence about whether we do or don't want to lead students out of what in our secret heart of hearts we perceive as their beautiful, prelapsarian ignorance of our pro- fessional infighting, all our uncertainty about truth and beauty and un-hold-onto-able meanings, all that knowledge about how lang- uage and power create truth. We don't know if we want to *expose* students (even the verb suggests knowledge-as-virus), because we aren't sure how we feel about having been exposed; about having fallen from paradise, or at least what in retrospect looks like paradise.

I want to suggest we consider that our student is really our Döppelganger; our other self; our Other. The student is our idealized Other when we see her or him as our unfallen self. For me the best moments in *Semiotics and Interpretation* come when its author wrestles with what it means to impart knowledge of the codes to students. At one point he muses over the recognition that becoming a participant in any discipline involves "giving up or sacrificing." If we impart new interpretive strategies, new "codes," what happens to the interpretive strategies and the codes with which students come into our class? Do we supplant them? Augment them? I maintain he isn't sure whether he wants them to acquire the information that will enable students to progress in formation. And neither are the rest of us. One reason for our mystifications—the way we teachers have a habit of revealing without revealing—is that we don't want to ruin our relationship to the student/Other. We *need* him.

Sometimes we see the student as our Idealized Other; sometimes the student is our most Despicable Other Self. Our exasperated exhalations at the awful laziness, lapses, stubborn resistances to learning, the stupid writing blocks we chide students for—and try to exorcise in conferences—are also our own, projected onto them. Successful projection, of course, first requires identification. Grading papers, especially that fiercer kind of red-lining we do, I suspect of being in part a kind of self-flagellation. It even produces the appropriate red marks. One of my colleagues is more revealing than he knows when he refers to that activity as "degrading papers."

Students and teachers are in a complicit relation. To use physicist David Bohm's wonderful book title, we are part of an "implicate order." That kind of awareness could help de-polarize pro-theorite and anti-theorite. It could also transform teaching. In the middle of the night, in what can only be explained as the fault of my hypnagogic state, I decided those awarenesses ought to be published under the title *Therapeutic Propadeutics*.

Recent appropriations of the word by teenagers notwithstanding, teaching really is awesome in its consequences and possibilities. It's no accident that it's easier for us to read Moliere's classroom than our own. It's no accident that in all of history the two most respected teachers have both, in a sense, been speechless speakers. Socrates and Jesus, both of them surely aware of the power in the pedagogical situation, left the writing of their texts to others.

So I applaud Professor Scholes' drive to give students access to codes and thereby to power. But insofar as he and the rest of us may still see teaching too much as a one-way street—impartation on the one hand and inculcation on the other—he may inadvertently help to preserve exactly those hierarchies he has fought his whole career to mitigate against. Thus, to his recent wonderfully astute question, "Is There a Fish in This Text?" which is itself a wonderful turn on Fish's "Is there a Text in This Class?" I'd like to see us add one more turn, and ask "Is there a *Class* in This Text?" with all the ambiguities in that formulation fully intended.

Richard Ohmann | Teaching as Critical Practice

First let me congratulate the Center for Literary Studies on setting this year's topic. As theory has become the privileged discourse in our major journals and at our conferences, a gap has widened between the language we use in those arenas and the language(s) we use in our daily practice. To be sure, some of us can and do teach unmediated theory, in seminars or advanced classes. But most of us spend most of our time teaching composition or literature—and that mainly to undergraduates. Should theory enter into that discourse? My answer is: Yes, sooner or later, one way or another; or the theory in question is void. I'm suggesting that theory "for its own sake" is a self-indulgent project of distinguishing ourselves from the ignorant laity. If anyone wants to reply that theory is the advancement of knowledge, I ask, "for whom"? Transmission of knowledge to students is no demeaning or special test to which humanists alone must submit; theoretical physics has the same goal. We all try to know the world, and keep that knowledge alive and growing by teaching it.

To my mind, we differ from the physicists mainly in the sort of thing we call theory, and in how we connect it to phenomena. Our theory is softer—I would be happy if we used the word "ideas," most of the time, instead of "theory"—and it is harder to detach from the things it is about, as is evident by the absence from it of mathematics. But in a way, those differences make it easier to teach. We can integrate it with the practice of reading texts, which is our equivalent of doing experiments and making observations. So I want to argue, today, mainly by sharing with you words I addressed to my students, in a course I recently taught on American fiction between the world wars, and by reflecting on those words. The point is not to claim that I have overcome the great difficulties of teaching as a critical practice, intermingled with theory. I have not; I am discontented with what I have done, in this as in every other course. But just as cultural and literary theory resist autonomous formulation, so do theories of the pedagogy of theory; and I can best get at what seem to me the issues by telling you what I try to do.

Specifically, I encourage students to read and ponder literature as part of the historical process, and in engagement with some ideas about history happens and how consciousness and culture interact with material life. My framework of ideas is marxist (and feminist—but I'll limit myself to the former, today). And of course I can assume no prior knowledge of these ideas, any more than I could if I were drawing upon semiotics or the theory of myth. Furthermore, "Modern American Fiction" is a period course, with the usual commitment to a fairly long list of novels, as well as readings in social, literary, and economic history. So there is no time for a leisurely study of theory. I have to invoke it as a kind of counter-point to other activities.

Needless to say, this stretches my attention and that of the students. I make it clear to them that we are embarked upon a large, messy project rather than a neat, encompassable one. For instance, at the beginning of the course, when I have assigned a brief excerpt from Terry Eagleton's *Marixsm and Literary Criticism*, I say to them—in writing, for reasons I'll explain later:

As Eagleton says, literature—and more broadly, consciousness—is part of a whole way of life built on and around the economic forces and relations that propel any society. So "To understand literature...means understanding the total social process of which it is part" (5-6). He soon acknowledges that "this may seem a tall order to the student of literature" (7); and I would drop the word "seem." It's not just a tall order, in fact; it's impossible. You can't comprehend a "total social process"; neither can I or anyone else. But this only means that we (you and I) are in the situation that *always* holds in humanities classrooms: we are trying to understand something infinitely complex—a world in which everything is connected to everything else. We are trying, that is, to do something we can never complete, or maybe even do very well. That's cause for modesty, but not for giving up the effort. Whatever we accomplish is better than nothing, certainly better than the blank ignorance about culture and history that is the air we breathe in this society.

Yet I do not begin by striving for the totalizing comprehension to which Eagleton refers. I start with something like close reading, but directing it toward an exploration of social and historical consciousness, working up to the point where I can bring Eagleton's discussion of ideology into focus. For instance, this is how I begin with Wharton's *The Age of Innocence*, our first novel.

To make the challenge less intimidating, it may help to start small, with some particulars about *The Age of Innocence*, taking it on (what seem to me) its own terms. This is not a general method—I *have* no general method—but a handy way to proceed at the beginning. So let me start by asking what consciousness the novel establishes, what kind of experience it asks you to become involved in.

You enter a world tightly circumscribed. The narrator calls it "the world of fashion" on p. 3, "society" on p. 5 ("never appearing in society without a flower...in his buttonhole"), and "New York" on pp. 1 and 8. The second and third of these names make clear what an exclusive consciousness you have come into. For these people, society *is* this small elite; New York *is* the "brilliant audience" assembled at the Academy of Music. (Have you heard of "the 400"? That was roughly the number that could fit into the ballroom of Mrs. William Backhouse Astor in the 1870s, so "the 400" became a nickname for the only people who counted.) You will not meet many people from outside this group, in *The Age of Innocence*. In Chapter 1, for instance, only one is mentioned, and that generally: "the cold-and-gin congested nose of one's own coachman" (4). A servant, a non-person—there only because he is needed by the people who count, and referred to contemptuously. As you read the novel, notice how—and how rarely—people outside the group appear.

And think about the other exclusions. The special world of the novel is a few square miles of Manhattan, along with a few places where "New York" goes for recreation: the great houses on the Hudson, Newport, St. Augustine, Paris, London. In between, there is nothing, just as there are no workers, no immigrants (though there are "foreigners"), no farmers (check out the one exception to this). There is virtually no *work*—we find out only on page 84 what Newland Archer's job is (some job!). Food, houses, dresses, silver, draperies, are just magically there, when needed by the wealthy. Think about what is and isn't included in the consciousness of the novel, in its "world." The scope is narrow.

Within that scope, values are also narrow, and rigid. Preserving "society" is high on the list, "keeping out the 'new people' whom New York was beginning to dread and yet be drawn to" (3). That has to do centrally with marriage and money, as you will find out in exquisite detail, and also with the usually-unspoken rules that govern the conduct of society. It is "not the thing" (4) to get to the Opera early; Newland understands the "duty" (5) of using two monogrammed brushes to part his hair; Lawrence Lefferts, the expert on "form," can "tell a fellow just when to wear a black tie with evening clothes and when not to" (8). More consequentially, the elaborate rules which govern relations between men and women are a main theme of the novel.

Given this consciousness and these values, you can predict that action itself will be narrowly defined in the novel, even before you discover that the climactic action of the first chapter is the appearance in Mrs. Manson Mingott's box of a young woman with the "Josephine look," and the reaction her entry provokes: "Well—upon my soul!" and "My God!" from Lefferts, and "I didn't think the Mingotts would have tried it on" from Sillerton Jackson. That such shock waves emanate from the Mingotts' decision to appear in public with a family member who has left her husband shows what small events count as big actions in this narrative. That this is the only significant event in eight pages suggests that the *meanings* of an action are more central to this novel than the action itself; and that ratio of act to commentary will hold throughout the novel— probably to the considerable impatience of some of you. By other standards, nothing much happens in this novel: invitations, visits, refusals, words said and not said, a wedding, a bank failure. Yet these are presented as tremendously meaningful.

Of course there's another part of the novel's consciousness, right from the start—the narrator's humor and satire. (Try to figure out how distinct this is from that of Newland Archer, whose point of view the narrator generally adopts.) It's quietly there from the outset: "remote metropolitan distances above the Forties'"; "excellent acoustics, always so problematic a quality in halls built for the hearing of music"; "democratic principles." It's a little more pointed in reference to the affair that had nearly ruined Mrs. Rushworth's life, and "disarranged [Newland's] own plans for a whole winter" (7). It supplies a steady perspective on the small moral universe of these people: Mrs. Manson Mingott, the boldest of them all, had "put the crowning touch to her audacities by building a large house of pale cream-colored stone...in an inaccessible wilderness near the Central Park," a house that remains as "visible proof of her moral courage" (13).

But we can't take this satire as the novel's main perspective. If we did, the novel would have only the slightest interest for most of us: OK, so these are trivial, self-important people with quaint mores; is that enough to keep us reading for 350 pages? (Not me.) Wharton's gentle mockery isn't the final word, because the novel's main characters are more generous and intelligent than what the satire mocks, and because the ethos of "New York" causes them pain and deprivation. One can mock the "system" (8), but one can't dismiss it, because it damages human beings. For instance:

1. It represses sexuality—for women more than men, but for men too; and even within marriage, since preparation for marriage desexualizes women and teaches men to expect the erotic only from "bad" women. This is too obvious for commentary. I'll just mention that one intelligent critic (Elizabeth Ammons, *Edith Wharton's Argument with America*) holds that "the subject" of this novel is "fear" of female sexuality, in the person of Ellen Olenska. I think that's too specific, but not bad.

2. The system deforms *all* relations between men and women. Again, no need for commentary, because after Newland's outburst—"Women ought to be free—as free as we are" (42)—Chapter VI begins with several pages of a devastatingly acute and explicit critique of patriarchy. (Read it now, if you haven't: do you think

Wharton fully endorses it? Is this a feminist novel? Why does Wharton give these insights to a *male* character?)

3. The system destroys honesty, because so much of human life is labeled "unpleasant" and hence undiscussable: "Does no one want to know the truth here, Mr. Archer?," asks Ellen (78). And Newland himself recognizes that he lives in a world "where the real thing was never said or done or even thought" (45). Very often, the key part of a dialogue is what Newland thinks, and wants to say, but does not (145, 232, 237, 295, and dozens of other examples). Several times, he is on the edge of saying the "real thing" and taking some responsibility for his life, but he can't, and when he can it's too late.

4. In short, the system badly impairs the self. Ellen wants to be "free" (e.g., 109, 111), but can't. No more can Newland. May not only can't, but "had not the dimmest notion that she was not free" (195). It's futile for Newland to burst out at her. "Original! We're all as like each other as those dolls cut out of the same folded paper. We're like patterns stencilled on a wall" (83). The rules and the power behind them have made the possibility of an untrammeled self as unattainable as it is desirable.

So the novel appeals to values far deeper than the sophisticated, "modern" ones carried along by the satire and humor. It appeals to values that are undoubtedly important to many of you, and if so, you have to care about what's at issue in the novel, that is, much more than a silly stuffiness that one can brush aside with a knowing gesture.

Well, if "Society" crushes its most decent members, is the presiding attitude of the novel one of resentment, rage, and good riddance? Pretty obviously not: the narrator (and Wharton, I'd say) finds this social milieu fascinating, even noble, as well as restrictive and foolish. Why? You'll find lots of answers as you read, but for an important one, please turn for a minute to the middle of p. 265, and read to the end of the chapter. The extraordinary translation, in the long paragraph on p. 266, of May Archer's brief sentence makes it as clear as anything in the book that the "hieroglyphic" code of this world is more than "a set of arbitrary signs" (45): it is a subtle instrument for expressing—and *living out*—the most complex meanings. The culture is not just hollow and fraudulent. It is a rich though flawed achievement of human beings living together over historical time. Its passing can occasion the same kind of sadness we might feel at the passing of any traditional society. Human variety and possibility have been diminished, and the loss is irretrievable.

Wharton explicitly encourages an anthropological perspective. Right at the beginning, New York's code of conduct is compared to "the inscrutable totem terrors that had ruled the destinies of his forefathers thousands of years ago" (4). We find (45) that people of "advanced culture" are beginning to read "books on Primitive Man"; Newland finds that "his readings in anthropology" (69) give him insight into the workings of his society. The wedding of Newland and May—the structurally central event of the novel, both in that it occurs just halfway through, and that all other events either lead up to it or proceed from it—is "a rite that seemed to belong to the dawn of history" (179), and secrecy about the location of the bridal night (sex, get it?) is "one of the most sacred taboos of the prehistoric ritual" (180). The language of totem and taboo, rite and ritual, tribe and clan, matriarch and patriarch, runs through the whole narration, climaxing in a terrifyingly polite ceremony at the Archers', which Newland understands as "the tribal rally around a kinswoman about to be eliminated from the tribe" (334). Of course most of this vocabulary suggests an unenlightened way of life; still, the loss of any culture diminishes us, and as Newland muses years later, "there was good in the old ways" (347).

Where does this anthropological consciousness come from? Is it the icily neutral distance of science? I think not. Partly, it comes from the historical distance Wharton and her readers (1920) would naturally feel, looking back on the early 1870s. More about that in the next non-lecture. But within the novel, too, this consciousness has perceptible links, not to a supposedly objective science, but to a way of life apart from that of New York society, and with claims and values of its own. Think again of the books on Primitive Man: who reads them? People of "advanced culture"—intellectuals? *Newland* reads them, and reads much else that is "advanced" (George Eliot, George Meredith, Nietzsche), as well as much that is old and beautiful. Why is Newland Archer fit to be the hero of this novel? He may flatter himself a bit in feeling superior to other members of the club, because of his having "read more, thought more, and even seen a good deal more of the world, than any other man of the number" (8), but again and again his Culture, capital "C", of poetry, fiction, philosophy, music, and art seems to qualify him for more refined feelings, and a broader perspective than the others. What has made Ellen Olenska so much wiser and freer and deeper a person than the other women? Her suffering, of course, but mainly her roots in the high culture of Europe, by comparison to which New York is a provincial backwater. What keeps "New York" that way? Partly its isolation from artists and "people who write," "the people among whom Ellen chooses—unfashionably—to live, on 23rd St. A cosmopolitan awareness is woven through the book, affording a breadth of vision to which New York society appears narrow, like a tribe at the dawn of history.

That awareness gains authority, also, from the only two characters in the novel who, though outside Society, are given some attention: Winsett, with his sad irony and his decent family life; and, much more important, M. Riviere. The latter's part is small, but he comes through as the only person in the novel who is—within limits set by his circumstances—both entirely honorable and his own free self. Check out the passage on p. 200, where Riviere articulates his philosophy: I don't think there's another passage in the book that gives such a glimpse of autonomy and liberation—and this good life is entirely bound up with books, ideas, the arts.

I'm suggesting that the ideal behind the anthropological view of New York, and behind the narrator's voice, is that of the free intellectual or artist, bound to no class or country, citizen of the republic of letters. (If so, that's not too surprising: such a person was Edith Wharton, or she tried to be; and after all, a novel is written by a novelist, who more than likely has her own professional ideology!)

Now, back to the beginning, and let me wind this up fast—it's already too long. I set out to explore the consciousness that we enter when we read *The Age of Innocence*. That turned out to be fairly complex. How might it be related to the "total social process" that Eagleton asks us to consider? Literature, he says, following Marx, belongs among the "forms of social consciousness" which overlay the productive base of a society. It is part of "ideology," that complex of beliefs and values and habits which makes the existing power relations of the society seem "natural," or invisible (4-5). He qualifies this in two ways: an ideology is a complicated and contradictory phenomenon (6-7), appearing differently in different classes and individuals; and art is not *just* ideology, but often a critical or subversive force, too (17-19).

Here's how I suggest viewing *The Age of Innocence*, against this background of ideas. On one level, the fiction stays within the ideology of New York's (capitalist) dominant class, *c.* 1875—accepts as limits its definition of people who count, its values, its customs, all the blinders that allow it a serene confidence in the propriety of its wealth, privilege, and power. But of course Wharton also permits us to "feel" and "perceive" this ideology, "thus revealing to us (its) limits" (Eagleton, 18-19). She does this through the satire of her narrator, through the troubled consciousness of Newland Archer, through the "anthropological" perspective, through the suffering that "New York's" ideology brings to characters we are supposed to care about. In spite of the nostalgia that enters the novel, I doubt that anyone reading it would come away thinking the Mingotts, Van Luydens, Leffertses, etc. a fit set of rulers for a society the reader would want to live in.

But beyond that is another level still, where the values reside by which that ruling class is found wanting. The free, untrammeled, unique, "original" individual, expressing itself freely (including sexually), above or outside of any particular society or set of institutions, free through ideas and literature and art and conversation: this is the ideal that the novel privileges—even though Wharton and her narrator concede that it is all but impossible to achieve. I've called this an ideology of writers and intellectuals, who stand apart from bankers and industrialists and stockbrokers and often bitterly criticize them. But this romantic ideal of the free self, I suggest, is critical of the capitalist world order only from a point of view internal to it; it is itself a form of capitalist ideology—of individualism, specifically, which has its base in the ideology of the free market and of free competition.

Think about it, and let's debate it in class.

Ideology is a key concept, and a notoriously vexed one; I have trouble with it; so do students. I return to it again and again through the course. It is the bridge between fictional texts and the historical process, impossible to understand through merely synchronic analyses like the one I have just excerpted for you. Students need to know something about economic and social history, and about class. To repeat, I ask them to read a variety of materials to help ground our discussion of novels and consciousness. But those readings would add up to little more than fragments, without something like an historical overview. I attempt that, from time to time, fully aware of how crude the attempt must be. Now I want to give you an extended example. In the lecture on *The Age of Inocence* I moved from text to theory; here, in a discussion of short fiction by Katherine Brush and James T. Farrell, and a novel by John Dos Passos, I move in the opposite direction.

Each of the four novels we've studied so far conveys a keen awareness of historical change. That awareness is virtually *the* subject of *My Antonia* and *The Age of Innocence*. It is strongly present in *This Side of Paradise* (in the explicit contrast between morals of the young and those of the parental generation), and implicit in *A Farewell to Arms* (in Frederic Henry's conviction that the vocabulary and the style he has inherited from the past will no longer do, because of the world-historical event he has lived through). In each of these novels, too, the presiding consciousness—Jim Burden's, Newland Archer's, Frederic Henry's, Amory Blaine's—is that of a relatively privileged and well-educated person. I believe that the awareness of history has something to do with this fact. In the stories by Farrell and Brush, and in the Charley Anderson sections at the beginning of *The Big Money*, the narrative point of view puts us inside minds that are less educated, belonging to characters of lower status; and there is little or no awareness that immediate events participate in wider movements and changes. So we have, among all these fictions, two contrasting perspectives. I'll try to explain that, in the course of the non-lecture.

Now, to the big picture, with apologies to those of you for whom it is old stuff. What brings about historical change, especially epochal change? Why does history happen? Marxists locate the answer to this question in *production*, the fundamental relationship of human beings to nature and to one another. To explain why, I return to the idea of *forces* and *relations* of production, mentioned all too briefly by Eagleton.

Forces of production include materials used in growing and making useful things; tools, machines, and (in our epoch) factories; and also skills, techniques, and knowledge—all the accumulated capabilities of the producers. Relations of production are the social structures and processes within which production takes place. In our epoch, for instance, they include the legal relationship of private property, processes for exchanging money and commodities, the boss-worker relationship, and many others. A central relation, almost the defining characteristic of capitalism, is that of the labor market, in which most people sell—as a *commodity*—their labor power, to an employer who will then extract their labor during the specified time of work. Another crucial relation concerns the social *surplus*: everything that is produced beyond the minimum necessary to maintain a stagnant society from one generation to the next. (In every non-stagnant society, there is conflict over possession and use of the surplus, sometimes muted and sometimes intense.) Most past societies have produced a surplus, but the ways in which it emerges and in which it is controlled differ sharply from one epoch to another. In capitalism, uniquely, the surplus emerges in the form of *profit*, and control of it partly defines the bourgeoisie, or capitalist class. This is another relation of production.

All right, change: forces of production are generally dynamic, as individuals and groups devise ways to produce more things or new things, or to cut down the labor required, and thus to better their material lives. Relations of production, by contrast, are conservative. Laws and institutions, for instance, fix in place relations of power and privilege, which the beneficiaries will hang onto in every way possible. So within any mode of production, a tension grows between new forces and old relations. Eventually, the class allied with the new forces asserts its dominance. This may happen gradually and without full-scale class war, as, in the Northern states, industrial capitalism outpaced the old "domestic" mode of production, and capitalists took control of the future from landowners and small farmers. Or it may happen suddenly and violently, as the Civil War abruptly ended the slave mode of production in the American South. (Need I add that every term and every sentence in this thumbnail sketch could be elaborated and disputed endlessly?)

These processes of change had, by the 1920s, brought to maturity a new mode of production which marxists usually call "monopoly capitalism" for reasons I won't go into now, and which others call "industrial capitalism," "advanced capitalism," and various other things. In this course we have given some attention to one aspect of this great transformation—the movement of people from farm to city, the dominance of city over country, and the establishment of city life as the norm.

In fiction, the city becomes the privileged site, the place to which the action moves, as with most of the novels in this course. It is a place where one mingles with strangers. Both Jack Stratton ("A Jazz-Age Clerk") and Mrs. Brady ("Night Club") exchange words with just one person previously known to them, but see and hear many notable strangers. Charley Anderson rattles around New York in isolation, touching base occasionally with the few people he really knows, moving from hotel to hotel. Locations like hotels become almost archetypal; "A Jazz-Age Clerk" takes place mainly in a hotel lobby, "Night Club" almost entirely in a powder room.

I'll now consider quickly some other main ways in which capitalism remade society, keeping tabs as I go on corresponding literary themes and modes of representation.

In capitalist society, most people come to be employees, working for wages and salaries. In 1800 a large majority of Americans worked for themselves, usually in family units on farms. By 1870, half the working population worked for others. I don't know the figure for 1920, but today over 90% work for others; let's guess that the proportion was about 75%

in the twenties. Going out to work meant that someone else owned and organized one's workplace and controlled one's productive time. If one's work helped make a product, that belonged to someone else, too. Increasingly, that someone did the planning and thinking. All this adds up to alienated labor.

Work becomes less and less a vital subject for fiction; notice how rarely it is so in our novels, except for those that have rural settings. Characters often hate the work available to them, as Charley Anderson does the idea of staying at his brother's Ford agency. (He wants less alienated labor, using his aircraft know-how, his creativity.) For Jack Stratton, "What he liked best about his job was his lunch hour..." (Ain't We Got Fun?, 352), and Mrs. Brady looks forward to her "recess" all evening (317). The boss is an alien and hostile figure. Jack is terrified that Collins will "bawl the hell out of him" (359) for being late; Mr. Costello's mere look makes Mrs. Brady almost run to her post in the powder room (307).

Production, the basis of all human life, becomes for most people a contaminated area.

Correspondingly, capitalism drives a wedge between workplace and home, work and leisure. With selfhood repressed at work, leisure is redefined as human time. Since this is the flip side of the previous point, I won't dwell on it, but wanted to mention it in passing. More about it in later non-lectures.

In capitalist society, almost all production is for exchange, not for use by the producers. The product disappears from the ken of workers, goes into the universal *market*, and there confronts the same workers as a commodity available for purchase. One lives by commodities, hence what one can purchase, hence money. Money in the form of wages also measures one's worth; one's labor power is itself a commodity with a certain value in money terms.

Notice how these stories linger on commodities, as signifiers of personhood. Money itself becomes a daily concern, a focus of desire, an inescapable adjunct to fantasy. Mrs. Brady accepts the slights and insults of the evening so that her seventy cents of "decoy money," arranged "in four-leaf clover formation" (!-308) will accumulate more; obsessed with money and the dreary work she does for it, she fails even to notice the human conflicts and crises that rage around her. For Jack Stratton, investing a hard-earned dime in a shoeshine might transform him into a big shot in the lobby of the Potter Hotel, and magically win a "ritzy queen" for him (355-56). Charley Anderson also sits in a hotel lobby, making the connection between money and sexual fulfillment; the silk stockings, high heels, and fur-coats give off an "expensive jingle and crinkle," and he starts "counting up how much jack he had" (37). Jim's and Hedwig's money-grubbing disgusts him, but he heads back to New York dreaming of success and an expensive woman (67-8). I think it's interesting how often, in the fiction of this time, money ties in with the most fundamental of all fantasies, sexual ones. Money also defines the free, satisfied self; all these characters identify their unfreedom with the lack of it. People must go shopping to survive, they are also coaxed and lured into markets.

Early, competitive capitalism spent its energies revolutionizing *production*, and let sales take care of themselves. This proved a risky business. Factories meant high fixed costs; they could run full-time without a lot more expense than it took to run them below capacity. The tendency was to keep the machines going, turn out the goods, and cut prices when necessary to push aside the competition. (A side-effect of this naive practice is worth mentioning: through the period of competitive capitalism, and up to about 1900, there was no long-term inflation at all.) That meant killing risk for individual companies, and for the whole economy a powerful drive towards "overproduction," which would be followed by cutbacks, layoffs, and bankruptcies—in other words, the devastating boom-and-bust cycle that characterizes our system. Gradually, toward the end of the last century, capitalists began to see that a solution lay in integrating *sales* with production. Rather than just make the goods, they would undertake nationwide distribution, creating in advance the markets for what they produced. That meant that they had to invent advertising; that in turn sponsored a mass, consumer culture. Capitalists colonized leisure, as they had assumed control of production.

Now, I just want to remark how the siren songs of mass culture sound through these stories. Jack Stratton's ideas and fantasies are little more than the internalization of popular song lyrics, and movie-made ideals. Mrs. Brady's magazine tells her stories that are more real than her real life, "live, vivid threads in the dull, drab pattern of her night" (318).

Corporations that took within themselves the entire process of production and distribution, in order to integrate and rationalize it and increase their stability, were necessarily large. Small ones tended to lose out and disappear, or were swallowed up by the more successful ones. (There were well over 2000 mergers in the last two years of the nineteenth century.) A fundamental law of capitalism is *grow or die*. These corporations—totally different in scope and structure from the older family businesses, and a new phenomenon in human history—increasingly took control of the decisions that shaped daily life and determined the future. But their control was remote, in two senses.

From any one geographical point in the U.S., most of them were distant and invisible. And even if you lived next door to the headquarters of a corporation, or worked in one of its factories or offices, you could not see how it organized the processes of production, or who made the decisions, or in what way; certainly you had no part in them unless you were a major exectuive or shareholder.

In effect, both the human activities of making things and the centers of social control became invisible. (Compare an eighteenth-century village, where practices of farming and craftsmanship were visible to all, and where, to the extent that a few men had power, other men and women knew exactly where it lay and how it was being used.) Monopoly capitalism is the most opaque mode of production and form of society, ever. Its workings are hidden. Ordinary people cannot see the springs of its power, though they know themselves not to share it.

In fiction, especially fiction about "little" people, this fact of the social order often appears in a sense of diminished scope and freedom for characters. We have "heroes" with little power to act, and with a narrow grasp of their situations. A trapped feeling emanates from the text in what Northrop Frye called the "ironic mode." We've seen this—even in the relatively well-positioned heroes of the first four novels: Jim Burden, drawn almost unwillingly into urban life; Newland Archer, enmeshed by the rules of "Society"; Frederic Henry, reduced to doing what feels right, but discovering that "they" will destroy you anyhow; Amory Blaine, stripped of his romantic ilusions. The feeling is much more overwhelming with characters like Jack Stratton and Mrs. Brady; their freedom of action hardly extends beyond getting a shoeshine or arranging coins in a saucer. They don't act; circumstances act through them.

Dos Passos conveys this helplessness pointedly; most of his characters get bumped along by forces within and without, which they barely understand, much less control. Look at p. 63 of **The Big Money,** *for a fairly typical example. Charley has been prisoner of his emotions at and after his mother's funeral. The next day, Emiscah asks him for a date. "Before he knew what he was doing, he'd said he'd come." He dislikes her and her life, but when she cries and asks for a kiss, he kisses her. He goes up to her apartment even "though it was the last thing he'd intended to do." She talks despondently, and Charley "had to pet her a little to make her stop crying"; then, aroused, he "had to make love to her." Charley is often on automatic pilot, when he's not yielding to someone else's will. He has a vague goal for himself, but no plans for achieving it; when his break eventually comes, it feels like magic.*

I want to make one more point about the economic and social system that emerged in the last century, matured in this, and is our own milieu. I've said it before, but it bears repeating. Capitalism makes us more and more interdependent, in a world-wide network of production and a worldwide market (not to mention a worldwide death machine). It gives us "socialized production," in the marxist sense of the term. At the same time, it permits to a few people "private appropriation" of the surplus, through profit. Laws, institutions, and beliefs have grown up to protect that central privacy, and have encouraged millions who get no profit to place an equally high valuation on privacy and independence. We see this everywhere—the private home, the suburb, the automobile, the "personal banker," the perfume that makes each user smell unique, the myth of equal opportunity, the me decade, the "diversity" of Wesleyan University. The contradiction of powerlessness and individual aspiration, the social and the private, was already intense in the 1920s. One place to look for it is in characters like Jack Stratton and Charley Anderson, drawn to visions of individual success even in the midst of the reality of daily helplessness.

I'm saying that many of these writers imaginatively render, through individual lives, some of the deepest and most abstract features of their social system, inluding precisely those features new to it. Some of the characters themselves are aware of their personal lives as part of historical change. Others are not. The very lack of historical perspective—that narrowness of vision that can't look beyond the next lunch hour or the next work break or the next drink—often signals that the character is one of the little people,—a member of the working class without class consciousness, a non-participant in history.

Of course the *writers* of these fictions know more than their little people; the reader is supposed to share that knowledge. One thing to ask yourself, as you read these and other fictions of the period, is what attitude writer and implied reader (intellectuals, of a sort) have toward these characters. It can range all the way from amused condescension to pained sympathy and even admiration. Tracing such attitudes can tell us a lot about the position of writers themselves within American society, and how they felt about that position.

I hope that the connections I make between literary representations and movements of history help both to animate the theory and give resonance to the texts. Part of the idea is to encourage making connections, thinking holistically. I want students to be able to see an epoch in an image. I'd like them to read a story as a system of meanings, a response to history, and an intervention *in* history. I don't know how successful this project can be, given the ahistorical premises of contemporary culture, not to mention those of the literary instruction that many students have had.

This brings me to the matter of students' own relations to texts, their involvement in reading, and their perceptions of the course itself as an institution. I think it important to problematize all these things. On the one side, students need to see their own responses as themselves social and historical, not as unassailably individual, much less as objectively professional (apprentice scholars, learning a Method). Here's the kind of thing I say to remind them of this aim, from time to time.

Digression: you have to care about the issues, but obviously you don't have to like the novel's way of representing them in a fiction. No one has to like any book, no matter how many critics and teachers say it's "great" or a "classic." The point of this course is not to get you to appreciate/like all the novels; there are some I don't much like myself. But what do you do with your reaction when you find yourself bored or contemptuous or antagonistic? I suggest making that the subject of inquiry. Remember that very many other people, in the nineteen-twenties and after, have hugely admired each of these novels. Ask why; and ask why you don't. Remember that boredom, like admiration, is a relation: a novel isn't simply boring—it bores you; a novel isn't simply great—people (who?) admire it. Exploring these relations is an important part of historical thinking about literature. If you find yourself hating a novel, take that as an invitation to learn something about yourself, as an historical being, with a class, a gender, a race, a particular background, as well as about other people who loved the same novel. (Also, keep reading; you've got to pass this course.)

Marxist teaching cannot leave the student reader outside of society and history; to do so would be by default to privilege the bourgeois self whose autonomy marxism challenges. No more can teaching, within this theoretical framework, take the syllabus or the literary canon as inevitable. Although canon formation is not my main emphasis in this course, I try to keep alive an awareness that we have received novels of the 1920s and 30s through a complex social process that assigns value to certain books and shunts others aside. The politics and economics of canon formation become a subject for me when I teach about novels that were quickly forgotten and later rediscovered, like *Daughter of Earth, Their Eyes Were Watching God, Miss Lonelyhearts,* and *Call It Sleep.* Why the "neglect"? What historical shifts prompted the rediscovery?

I also remind students of this process when teaching about novels that were celebrated when new. Celebrated by whom? Here is a digression on novel buying and reading, from my non-lecture on *This Side of Paradise:*

Digression: Success is success, by the irrefutable measures of sales figures and profit. But it's important to keep in mind that "the book-buying public" was and is a small minority of the whole population. Wharton's novel was a blockbuster with sales of 115,000. This Side of Paradise, *a novel that "everyone" read and talked about, sold 40,000 copies in the first year and 70,000 by 1924. (Similar figures can put a novel on the hard-bound Best Seller List today, with the U.S. population more than twice what it was in 1920.) Suppose that each copy of a novel was read by three people, on average. Then a novel with sales of 100,000 had an audience consisting of three-tenths of one percent of the population. A tiny fraction, compared to the forty million who tuned into* Amos'n'Andy *each night on the radio, by the end of the decade. Yet from such publishing successes, along with critical acclaim, novels like these have become "classics," and, as part of "Modern American Fiction," appear on college syllabi in 1984. Think about this cultural process, and about the authority in it of a relatively few people. Who were they?*

And how did novels enter into the arena of cultural discourse in the first place? I try to touch on this question, too, *en passant.* For instance, while discussing the pertinence of *The Age of Innocence* to its time, I work back to the decisions that brought it into being, and into print.

It may seem that *The Age of Innocence* was an anachronism in 1920—not really of that time. A curious incident supports such a view: although Wharton's novel won the Pulitzer Prize in 1921, the jury had actually named another novel, Sinclair Lewis' *Main Street,* feeling that it had more contemporary relevance than *The Age of Innocence.* But the trustees (of the Pulitzer fund and of Columbia University) overruled the jury, apparently on grounds that *Main Street* gave offense to "a number of prominent persons in the Middle West" as Wharton put it in response to a sportsmanlike letter that Lewis wrote her. (This and much other information I'll draw upon comes mainly from R.W.B. Lewis' fine biography of Wharton.)

Still, Wharton did win the prize, and readers of 1920 gave a more telling verdict by buying over 100,000 copies of the book and making it a major best seller, while critics and reviewers praised it. The book was very much part of the cultural and commercial scene in 1920; in fact, its very genesis was commercial. In April, 1919, the editor of *Pictorial Review* offered Wharton $18,000 for serialization of her next novel. She jumped at the money (though she was hardly poor, with an inherited annual income of about $25,000 a year), and offered her novel-in-progress, *A Son at the Front*. Both the magazine editor and her publisher discouraged this, feeling that the public was tired of war novels. So she cooked up a scenario for a novel to be called "Old New York" (in which "Langdon Archer" and "Clementine Olenska" would spend a "few mad weeks" together in Florida, before returning to their routine lives). Publisher and magazine editor said fine, Wharton got the $18,000 plus a $15,000 advance on royalties, and she set to work. So the story had "contemporary relevance" in a crucial sense: men with the cultural and financial power to make such decisions bet that it would please the public, and they were right. Something in it spoke to the experience and needs of book-buying Americans in 1920.

For the last century, culture itself has been importantly a commercial process. To take note of that fact helps complicate crude ideas of base and superstructure within marxist theory. At the same time, it demystifies the academic category of "modern American fiction," and my syllabus itself.

For marxism demands critical reflection on the processes of its own transmission, as on everything else. Hegemony exists in course catalogues, in syllabi, in the conventions of teaching, in the architecture of the classroom, in the institution of college. If critical theory leaves these things unexamined, it falls shorts of its purpose, whatever insights it may promote into literature and history. To question one's own profession and practices is, of course, the hardest task of all. I don't know how successful I have been in this. But—without opening up, here, the educational controversies of the 1960s and after—I want in closing to say how I tried to interrogate the lecture system in Modern American Fiction.

I have mentioned that these lectures were written out. I called them "non-lectures," because I never delivered them orally. Instead, I distributed each one, a week or so in advance of the date on which I might have given it. When the class met, I did not begin the proceedings. There were six TA-led discussion and study groups (total enrollment was about fifty-five). One of the groups was responsible for a presentation, for initiating a dialogue, for somehow making the class happen. I was there, to participate in whatever role the TA group designated, or to respond to and develop what it had done. Sometimes I ended up being little more than an observer, as when one group did a well-researched demonstration of twenties radio, music, dancing, and advertising. Sometimes I turned out to be a main participant, when, for instance, a group decided to formulate questions about and challenges to my non-lecture—or, more amusingly, when they cast me as Miss Lonelyhearts, and delivered me a small packet of letters like the ones in West's novel, to which I had to respond extempore. There were surprises; there were classes that floundered. But we persisted, and I think that most students gained confidence that they could take some responsibility for their education even in a so-called lecture course. And as Marx would have it, the educator got educated.

I could go on, but will leave off with a few words about the politics of such teaching, addressed mainly to those of you who, like myself, are persons of the left. We who took part in sixties movements and became socialists, feminists, and (some of us) marxists along the way can take satisfaction from the renewal of American marxism since then. Those who do marxist scholarship have no cause to feel lonely now. There are thousands of us, at least according to an alarmed bourgeois press. We have our conferences and journals, and many presses welcome our books. Graduate students, even in conservative departments, usually learn that marxism has things to say, things which may be refuted but not simply ignored as in the intellectual darkness of twenty years ago. In this context, American marxists are contributing their share to a worldwide elaboration of theory and analysis. So far so good.

The danger I see in our present circumstances is a *new* kind of isolation. Acceptance in the academy came to us just as the movements that had fueled our thinking were breaking up, losing steam, changing direction. So our respectability (precarious and partial, of course) coincides with our greater distance from vital popular movements; cynics might say that the latter explains the former. Trustees and administrators can congratulate themselves on harboring critical thinkers, so long as they produce scholarly articles and an enhanced reputation for the university rather than strikes and sit-ins. I'm concerned that we may become *harmlessly* respectable. I'm also concerned that out marxism may become attenuated and abstract, a theory among other theories, a new marxology.

Teaching is not organizing—usually. But it is engagement with people other than ourselves, many of whom are open to new (and old) ways of understanding the world. We shouldn't put theory aside during these workaday encounters; nor can we assume that it will teach itself, via the conventions of the traditional classroom. We should be figuring out how to mediate it in ways that estrange those conventions. The language we use, and, yes, even the arrangement of the chairs, can make a difference.

List of Works Cited in the "Non-lectures"

Ammons, Elizabeth. *Edith Wharton's Quarrel with America*. Athens: U of Georgia P, 1980.

Brush, Katherine. "Night Club." *Ain't We Got Fun?: Essays, Lyrics, and Stories of the Twenties*. Ed. Barbara H. Solomon. New York: New American Library, 1980.

Cather, Willa. *My Antonia*. 1918; rpt. Boston: Houghton, n.d.

Dos Passos, John. *The Big Money*. 1936; rpt. New York: New American Library, 1969.

Eagleton, Terry. *Marxism and Literary Criticism*. Berkeley and Los Angeles: U of California P, 1976.

Farrell, James T. "A Jazz-Age Clerk." *Ain't We Got Fun?: Essays, Lyrics, and Stories of the Twenties*. Ed. Barbara H. Solomon. New York: New American Library, 1980.

Fitzgerald, F. Scott. *This Side of Paradise*. 1920; rpt. New York: Scribner's, n.d.

Hemingway, Ernest. *A Farewell to Arms*. 1929; rpt. New York: Scribner's, 1982.

Lewis, R.W.B. *Edith Wharton: A Biography.* New York: Harper, 1975.

Wharton Edith. *The Age of Innocence.* 1920; rpt. New York: Scribner's 1968.

William E. Cain | *Response*

I have many complaints to register about academic literary study, but I have to concede—and do so with pleasure—that criticism and scholarship are, in certain respects, in excellent shape. There are, to be sure, faults, defects, blind spots in the work that members of our discipline produce, particularly, in my view, the inert exchanges of Derridean and Lacanian jargon to which some post-structuralists are addicted, and also the breezily uncritical invocation of "disciplinary" rhetoric to which some of Foucault's followers seem to be drawn. But I can, more positively, very quickly begin to compile a list of impressive editions, translations, and monographs, all of which display—whatever divergences exist in authorial temperament and methodology—admirable ambition, intelligence, and analytical skill.

I have in mind, for example, W. J. Bate's and James Engell's dauntingly erudite edition of Coleridge's *Biographia Literaria*; Barbara Johnson's meticulous rendering into English of Derrida's highly formidable text, *Dissemination*; Sandra Gilbert and Susan Gubar's feminist literary history, and Nina Baym's and Elaine Showalter's wide-ranging recovery and discussion of nineteenth-century novels written by women; Jane Tompkins's treatment, in her *Sensational Designs*, of the sentimental tradition in American fiction; Eric Sundquist's provocative study of racial themes in Faulkner's novels; Don E. Wayne's inter-disciplinary interpretation of the poem and the place named "Penshurst"; Helen Vendler's deep soundings of the language of modern and contemporary poetry. And—to turn to today's speaker—Professor Ohmann's stimulating research, in the Autumn 1976 and September 1983 issues of *Critical Inquiry*, on canon-formation; his plain-spoken assessments of the social, economic, and political contexts for criticism; and, in *English in America: A Radical View of the Profession*, his pioneering (and still undervalued) examination of academic professionalism.

I also have in mind—to refer next to forthcoming books— Michael McKeon's richly contextualized inquiry into the origins of the English novel; Cathy N. Davidson's parallel exploration of the beginnings of the American novel; Evan Carton's unfolding of the "dialectics of romance" in the writings of Hawthorne, Poe, and other American masters; and Gerald Graff's survey of the development of English studies in America.

This mustering of names and projects might understandably strike some people as arbitrary, but in a way this is much to my point. There is, I think, a great deal of interesting, adventurous work being undertaken by critics and scholars in English and in foreign language departments, and most people can readily supplement the list I have assembled or else sketch a different yet equally imposing one.

However, trouble arises, or at least seems to arise, when we ask what coordinates and interconnects these various critical and scholarly achievements. At first glance, they appear to confirm Graff's suggestion that deconstruction is not at odds with contemporary literary study, but instead personifies it, with the "incommensurable vocabularies" of criticism perfectly embodying the endless contradictions and inconsistencies that deconstruction trumpets.[1] Perhaps, too, the discordant grouping of texts on my list bears witness to Ohmann's charge, in *English in America* and in his essay on "the social relations of criticism," that critics "produce" criticism but cannot necessarily explain and justify it, specify how its multiple forms cohere, or identify how its "use value" reaches beyond the closed circle that critics themselves create.[2] But while I judge these claims to be keen and valid to an extent, my angle of approach today differs somewhat from Graff's and Ohmann's.

At the risk of seeming to offer a cunning or tedious distinction, I would like to propose that criticism—"criticism" in the sense of critical and scholarly publication—is not defective or blundering or even excessive, but rather that its energies seem not to have effected much productive change in teaching and curricular structure—have not, that is, made much change in increasing the general production of minds devoted to critical thinking. One way, admittedly loose and impressionistic, of making my point is to say that sterling critical writing abounds yet Ronald Reagan is President and many students support him enthusiastically, and to observe additionally that criticism, scholarship, and theory are growing increasingly sophisticated and challenging even as American society descends into selfishness and profoundly callous disregard of its homeless, sick, and suffering.

As teachers, we do not succeed very well in encouraging students to think critically, and by this I mean to highlight the relation (or lack of relation) between critical practice in the classroom and critical thought in general—critical thought about the American scene and the world in which students (and their teachers) live. I may be an exception, but at moments in my day-to-day teaching, conferences, committee meetings, and the like, I feel I am less a teacher/critic who promotes and conveys the intensities of "criticism" than a diligent fellow in a glorified employment agency, one engaged in handing out credentials and easing young people's movement into the fast-lane of lucrative careers. I do not mean these words to sound bitter, and certainly do not wish to inveigh against my students (though this is sometimes a temptation), so many of whom are bright, earnest, hard-working, and driven by the anxieties and demands that American society unremittingly generates. Rather, I make these points about the inadequacies of our teaching more in a bemused, if also inquisitive, spirit, and do so with a sense of the complicatedness of the interwoven problems that mar teaching and that interfere with a truly forthright oppositional and resistant kind of critical thinking.

Let me try to be more specific. When I read college and university catalogues, I am often led to imagine that I could improve upon the curricula that the departments of English in these institutions have devised. But no sooner do I begin mapping ways to make each curriculum more rigorous, orderly, amd worldly in its orientation than I recall, from my own experience at Wellesley, that such local adjustments frequently collide with enrollment and budgetary necessities: if you seek really to organize the curriculum, impose requirements, and transform the major into something serious and integrated, you risk losing students and threaten to fracture your own department. Or, to take a second example, if you devise courses and programs that trespass on the texts and methods—and the students—of other departments, you may seem to be a divisive, self-serving soul who is not properly honoring the segmented constituencies and disciplinary boundaries that enable all (or most) within the institution to survive and prosper. Any reform is applauded, it sometimes seems, so long as it does not imperil enrollments or jeopardize someone else's fiefdom.

We might want at some later time to scrutinize in further detail the departmental and institutional limits to possible improvements in teaching, but in the space I have left, I want briefly to advocate several recommendations that can accompany our response to Professor Ohmann's paper. First, I would urge a renewed emphasis in teaching (and in criticism and scholarship as well) on evaluation—making and defending value judgments ourselves and encouraging students to do the same. Professor Ohmann has argued, correctly, that "to posit standards is always to engage in an ideological maneuver, to generalize the interests and values of one class or group and present them as the interests and values of all"; and he has elsewhere reminded us, in a similar vein, that "excellence is a constantly changing, socially chosen value."[3] But it is possible, I believe, for me to accept these insights and still contend for greater stress on evaluation, for seeing the act of interpreting texts as bound up with critical preferences, choices, decisions, responsibilities. Evaluation does not have to imply closure; it can be a process of debate and exchange, one in which class interests and values are openly expressed, challenged, and modified.

Second, I would like to dramatize the relationship—this is less a proposal than a topic for discussion—between value judgments and the recent expansion—which I welcome—of the canon. I think it is crucial that texts by women and minorities should become objects of literary study. Could one honestly teach a course on the American Renaissance, for example, without delving into the writings of Frederick Douglass, Harriet Beecher Stowe, and Margaret Fuller? My own inclination, then, is to strive for ever-greater catholicity and inclusiveness. But at least in teaching, I also wonder whether we do in fact need to be more strict about defining and limiting the field of texts, in part out of sheer pedagogical necessity—we cannot discuss all the relevant and important texts in a single semester. Perhaps we should make our choices, and in line with my stress on communal acts of analysis and judgment, view one of the concerns of the course to be investigating what the inclusions and exclusions of the reading-list imply.

This solution is helpful, but is not wholly satisfactory to me. Recently I received a copy of the Norton Anthology of American Literature (second edition), volume 1 totalling 2535 pages and volume 2 running to 2652 pages. Both include, as they should, minority and women writers, and hence testify to praiseworthy openness on the part of the editors. But neither cuts back at all, so far as I can tell, on the sizeable sections given to Hawthorne, Melville, Whitman, and the other male members of the traditional pantheon. Is this really inclusiveness or a characteristic form of American inflation, in which the editors offer more choices but default on discriminating among the range of choices? Does this signify a splendid pluralism or confess the impossibility of judgment—as though there were no basis for selection at all? I know I am being somewhat harsh, but what we have here are two massive books, both of which affirm bulk rather than critical thought, and both of which, whatever their copiousness, nevertheless still omit significant figures (William Lloyd Garrison and Randolph Bourne, for instance) and thus could be said—this is the nettling irony—to remain too restrictive. These books are big, but not big enough, and not necessarily better, despite laudable diversity in content, than what we have used in the past.

Ideally, books like the Norton Anthology might serve as a resource, as an opportunity for members of departments and students to join in colloquia about judgment-making and canon-formation. Most departments, possibly in an effort to avoid internecine war, hesitate to move beyond the isolated classroom and shun public forums, as if to admit that it would be upsetting to argue and disconcerting for students to observe disputes among the usually monolithic faculty. But we could benefit from much more debate and discussion within the department (and within the college or university), and also from much more explicit emphasis upon the social and political assumptions, values, and commitments of teachers. Students need to see the force—and maybe, too, the indignation—of criticism, and should recognize its significance as an act—to quote from Professor Ohmann's lecture—of "social and historical consciousness." They can only profit from witnessing and taking part themselves in general exchanges about literature, society, and culture, exchanges in which conservative and liberal, as well as radical, voices resolutely speak. I myself basically agree with the marxist slant of Ohmann's approach, though I suspect I place less faith in Marx himself and more in an American tradition (laced at key junctures with marxism) of radicals and reformers—Douglass, Garrison, DuBois, Bourne, Burke, and others—than he does. But I would also advocate very different kinds of approaches, not because I harbor a secret desire to disarm the left and dissolve its provocations into a slack pluralism, but rather because I see the immediate need to be the active encouragement of open debate, forthright speech about criticism and politics, higher education and the requirements of the marketplace. I would want to push for a vigorous, competitive inter-animation of voices.

Debate and dialogue of this kind is not easy to accomplish in contemporary literary and political culture, and an appeal for an enlargement of pedagogy in these directions may seem foolish and futile, as if—in Empson's words—"one hungers for greater absurdity." But have we so little faith in our powers of communication and persuasion, and such doubt in our ability to tolerate opinions different from our own, that we cannot imagine the potent value and excitement of occasions such as these? The curious truth is that while individual members of our discipline are themselves often contentious, especially when haggling about literary theory, the departmental and curricular structure of our work functions to mute or muffle conflict and deny dialogue, and colleagues, as Ohmann points out in *English in America*, thus make shockingly little use of each other *as* "colleagues," as fellow-teachers and intellectuals.[4] I eagerly seek ways to improve my own performance in the classroom, but also suspect that I would do even better to conceive of cooperative ventures, involving faculty, students, and anyone else, that occur outside the boundaries of the classroom or lecture hall. Here, I would want not only to assent to, but also to amplify, Ohmann's effort, as stated in today's lecture and other writings, to get faculty and students involved in critical thinking about the terms and tenets of education—its forms, valorized texts, institutional structures. Students today are admirably receptive but dismayingly unreflective, and we are far too cautious—largely because of departmental and institutional codes of conduct and pervasive systems of decorous restraint—about actively unsettling their mental habits and challenging ourselves to break with routine.

Notes

1. Gerald Graff, "Cultural Criticism and Co-Optation," p. 12. Unpublished manuscript.

2. Richard Ohmann, *English in America: A Radical View of the Profession* (New York: Oxford University Press, 1976), pp. 3-22, and "The Social Relations of Criticism," in *What Is Criticism?* ed. Paul Hernadi (Bloomington: Indiana University Press, 1981), pp. 189-98.

3. Ohmann, "The Social Relations of Criticism," p. 197, and "The Social Definition of Literature," in *What Is Literature?* ed. Paul Hernadi (Bloomington: Indiana University Press, 1978), p. 96.

4. Ohmann, *English in America,* p. 18.